Meridians

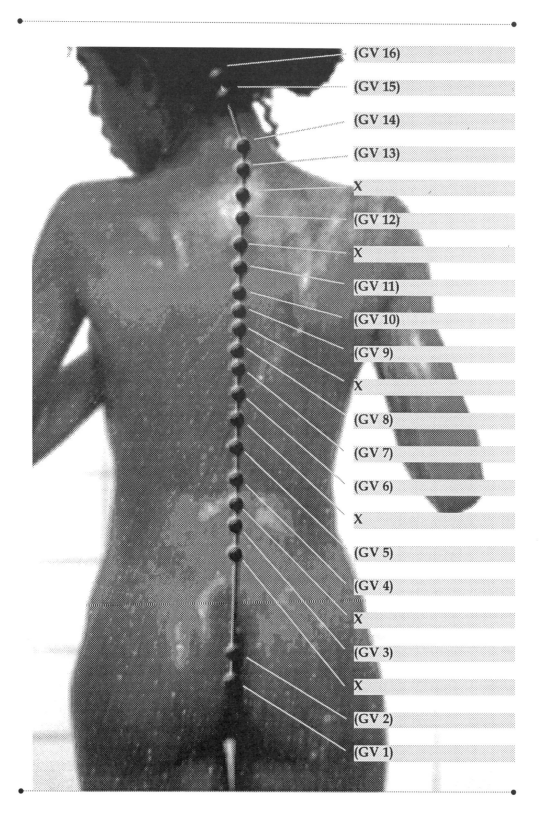

(GV 16)

(GV 15)

(GV 14)

(GV 13)

X

(GV 12)

X

(GV 11)

(GV 10)

(GV 9)

X

(GV 8)

(GV 7)

(GV 6)

X

(GV 5)

(GV 4)

X

(GV 3)

X

(GV 2)

(GV 1)

Astrolog ◆ The Quality of Life Series

Meridians

Tsao Hsueh-Lien and Bruce Thornton

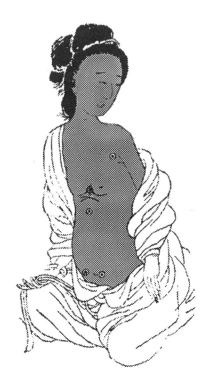

Astrolog Publishing House Ltd.

Cover Design: Na'ama Yaffe
Language Consultants: Carole Koplow
Layout and Graphics: Daniel Akerman
Production Manager: Dan Gold

P. O. Box 1123, Hod Hasharon 45111, Israel
Tel: 972-9-7412044
Fax: 972-9-7442714

© Astrolog Publishing House Ltd. 2004

ISBN 965-494-150-3

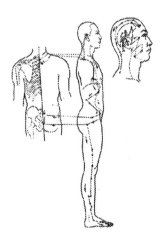

Published by Astrolog Publishing House 2004

Contents

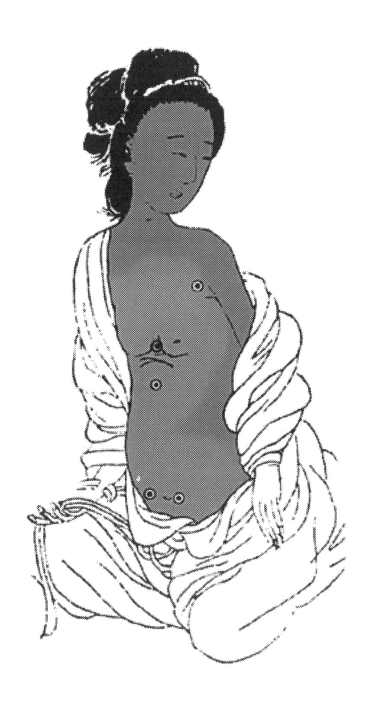

Introduction

Chinese medicine

In order to understand Chinese medicine and its influences on the West – with methods such as acupuncture, massage, and natural healing – we must first learn a few things about the culture of China.

First, the most important thing for us to remember is that Chinese medicine, as it exists today, has about 4,000 years of experience! If the Chinese physician of 2,000 years ago were to come to life today, he would easily fit into today's Chinese medicine.

It is important to remember that not only is Chinese medicine based on 4,000 years of experience, but also on the actual healing of hundreds of millions of Chinese! In other words, it is a method that has been successfully applied to countless cases over a long time.

Chinese medicine is based on a philosophy of life that is completely different to that of modern medicine in the West. However, we tend to think of Chinese medicine as traditional, alternative, "other" – in contrast to conventional modern Western medicine.

We should wipe this view out of our minds. These are two diverse methods of medicine with the same objective: life without disease (Chinese medicine) and curing disease (modern medicine).

Has modern Western medicine not undergone dramatic changes during the course of the last century? One hundred years ago, Western medicine used mainly medicinal herbs and homeopathic remedies, but today they are off-limits in conventional medicine! One hundred years ago, natural medicine was widespread in the West – natural living, organic food, and so on – while today, this kind of medicine is considered, in many cases, an escape from modern medicine. Even medicine based on faith or healing was widespread in the past; today it has no place in modern medicine.

Medicine in the West has become a matter of laboratories, chemicals, and state-of-the-art equipment. Gone are the days when the physician administered the treatment that was most appropriate for the patient, regardless of what area of medicine it belonged to. Today, diseases are treated, not the patients!

However, in modern medicine, too, there are many changes. Once, it was routine to extract children's tonsils; today, every effort is made not to do so thanks to the discovery of the important function of the tonsils in the immune system. Once, appendectomies were performed at the slightest excuse; today, every effort is made not to remove the appendix.

The truth is that in the West, as in the East, the same criterion is applied to all the methods: are they effective? We use aspirin extensively because it is effective... even though we cannot understand where its effectiveness comes from!

In addition, physicians in the West, after years of experience, are also opting to use the various methods of medicine. They are learning to know, for instance, that healthy nutrition prevents certain diseases, and therefore they recommended nutritional changes as a treatment. They are using the same method the Chinese have been using for thousands of years: if the method keeps the person healthy, it is effective!

Thus, we have to understand that Chinese medicine emerged in a different culture, from a different philosophy, and created a completely different method from that in the West – and this method works!

A person in the West who goes to a specialist for treatment with cupping glasses on his back is considered old-fashioned, not modern. A Chinese person who goes for similar treatment is not in the least exceptional – that's what was done thousands of years ago, and that's what's still done today. The important question is: Are cupping glasses effective? Does the treatment help?

It is important to remember two factors concerning China – time and quantity. The Chinese culture, which has already endured for six thousand years, has led to the belief that old and new are one continuous current in time. If we found a diamond a millennium ago, is it considered old-fashioned today? The second, equally important, factor is quantity. Since there are hundreds of millions of Chinese, the entire population serves as a gigantic laboratory in which various medical and healing methods can be "tried out."

Somebody once calculated that if all the Chinese arranged themselves in threes and marched towards a certain line, the rows of people would never come to an end. The newborns would always fill the rows! Understand this concept of size and you will understand the power of Chinese medicine.

Even today, with Western medicine penetrating China, a developed and effective system of Chinese medicine exists in parallel, and every Chinese person can choose his physician. The simple fact remains that Chinese medicine is no less effective – and sometimes more so – than Western medicine in China.

The philosophy behind Chinese medicine is different from that of Western medicine. In the West, we "fight" disease, we "wipe out" the epidemic, while in China, they see life as a part of nature. The person lives in harmony with nature, and disease attests to an upset of balance, a disruption of the harmony. The physician's role is to restore the balance and compatibility between man and nature – not to "fight" it.

This approach stems from the Eastern concepts of yin and yang – two essences that exist in everything. Everything is yin and yang. Yin is cold, dark, nocturnal, hollow, female. Yang is hot, light, diurnal, solid, male. Yin is negative, yang is positive. Inhaling and exhaling, falling asleep and waking up, heaven and earth, winter and summer – everything is yin and yang.

Thus, the body's organs were also divided into yin and yang. Hollow organs such as the lungs, the liver, and the kidneys are yin, while the stomach, the intestines, and the excretory system are yang.

Yin is not preferable to yang, nor is yang preferable to yin. They are not given values – they are simply different from each other. What really counts is the balance between them. Everything depends on the correct balance – the course of the stars, the raising of crops, the birth of children… everything in nature. When the yin and the yang are balanced and in complete harmony, everything "succeeds" – the crops are abundant, the newborn is healthy. Unfortunately, when the balance is upset, everything goes wrong: crops wither, the child is ill, and troubles mount up.

No phenomenon is entirely yin or yang. Everything contains both yin and yang, and the balance is the important thing. When the balance is upset, a yin phenomenon can become yang, and vice versa. This is not a desirable situation.

It is important to remember that yin and yang have no power – they are simply essences. It is other factors that upset the balance between them and cause problems.

Let us suppose that you have a bowl of blue paint on your table. The blue paint is a phenomenon. Within the blue paint there is a special balance of yin and yang, a balance that causes the blue to be blue. Now we will pour a factor, yellow paint, into the bowl. What will happen? The balance of yin and yang has been upset, and the phenomenon, the blue paint, will become green. Now the physician must diagnose what caused the imbalance (the factor – yellow paint), and determine the treatment that is required in order to balance the yin and yang, thus ensuring the return of the blue paint (let's say, by adding purple paint to the bowl).

Remember this example – this is exactly how Chinese medicine views the human body, the causes of diseases, and the role of the diagnosing and treating physician.

When yin and yang are in a state of balance in the human body, the person is in a state of good health. When the balance is upset, one or other part of the body does not function properly, and the person is considered to be ill. The physician's role is to restore the proper balance in the body.

In order to do so, the physician can select various methods: acupuncture, massage, medicinal herbs, cupping glasses, cold or hot baths, a diet, reflexology, and many others. All these methods are at the physician's disposal.

The patient is not considered to be a self-standing entity. His being ill, just as when he is healthy, is part of the forces of nature that surround him – and it is also the reason why the Chinese physician has to take into consideration the season, day, and hour that he examines the patient. Some are also in the habit of checking the patient's astrological map before making a diagnosis.

Chinese medicine, on the one hand, is an intuitive method, that is, the physician does not send findings to the laboratory for diagnosis, but rather makes the diagnosis himself. However, on the other hand, it is a method with an amazingly extensive system of rules and laws. This method deals mainly with the flow of the life force – *chi* – in the person.

Chi currents pass through the human body in channels, just like the blood or the electrical impulses in the nervous system. However, chi is not a liquid like blood, nor is it electrochemical as in the nervous system. It is impossible to see, feel, taste or smell chi, or touch it in a physical sense. Nevertheless, it exists in the human body, and its paths are fixed.

Perhaps we can understand this better if we speak about a flow of energy in the human body, as is the case in the West. It will be clearer, even though chi is not exactly an energy in the Western sense.

Chinese medicine deals mainly with the normal flow of chi in the human body. When the flow is disrupted, it is because the yin and the yang are no longer balanced.

Good health exists only when the chi flow is normal. The physician's role is to remove the obstacle and to restore the flow.

Chi moves through the body in channels, systems of channels, meridians, or "networks" (similar to the circulatory or nervous systems). There are 12 networks on each side of the body, and each one is linked to a certain part of the human body.

In addition to the 24 networks – a dozen on the right side of the body and a dozen on the left side – there are two networks at the center of the body, one at the front and one at the back.

As soon as a problem has been diagnosed and the affected organ identified, the physician treats one or another point on one of the meridians that is linked to that organ.

This is how acupuncture, massage, or the rest of the methods available to the Chinese physician work – diagnosis of the problem, identification of the meridian, and specific treatment of the point of blockage.

Initially, there were 365 acupuncture points, in accordance with the solar year. Today, about 600 additional points that were discovered during the hundreds of years of application have been added. Acupuncture originated in the Chinese imperial army about 5,000 years ago. The art of writing was highly developed in China, and every military division maintained records of every battle injury and its outcome. These records were stored in the imperial archives. The cases of soldiers who had been wounded in the leg by an arrow, for instance, and as a result of their injury had been cured of some other ailment such as diarrhea or a cough, were prominent in these records. As the testimonies became more numerous, the physicians began to look for the link between arrow wounds and the phenomena following them. The large number of imperial soldiers and the detailed accounts of every injury led to the writing of the Nai-ching, *The Yellow Emperor's Book of Internal Medicine*, about 4,000 years ago. From then on to this day, the book has served as the principal textbook for every Chinese physician.

The extent of the wisdom in the book can be illustrated by the simple fact that the circulatory system was described in full thousands of years before it was recognized and documented in the West (and at a time when dissection of corpses was totally prohibited in China)!

Today, too, the Nai-ching serves as the most important medical textbook in China, and most of its findings are still as correct as they were thousands of years ago!

In order to understand why this art was preserved for thousands of years without being challenged, we must remember that the Easterner, because of his belief in reincarnation, must be buried with all his organs intact: it is forbidden to amputate a sick organ or to dissect corpses. In fact, the Chinese learned about the human body from the outside, without penetrating it. Had they performed autopsies, they would have searched for the chi "networks" but would not have found them, of course. Perhaps this would have undermined their belief in acupuncture, and they would have looked for other methods of medicine. However, since they did not perform autopsies and did not seek the meridians in the body, they preserved the ancient art. They had an effective medical method at their disposal, and they developed it, exercising their senses of sight, hearing, smell, and so on, in order to use it.

The Chinese physicians spent thousands of years of trial and error developing their ability to diagnose and heal. The difficult conditions under which they worked must be remembered.

The physician was forbidden to see a woman from a noble family naked; in many cases, in fact, he did not see her at all. He would give her maidservant a doll, "a physician's doll," which the servant would give to her mistress. The latter would then mark the place where it hurt on the doll. The physician was supposed to cure her according to the mark! In many other cases, too, the physician was forbidden to touch the patient, while in certain cases he would touch the patient's face or hands. Thus, the physician had to learn about the patient's disease from information that was unfamiliar even to physicians in the West.

The Chinese physician has to diagnose the patient using four methods: sight, hearing, interview, and touch.

Using **sight**, the physician examines the patient by looking him over, discerning skin color and scrutinizing his nose, mouth, eyes, and mainly his tongue extensively. Every shade of color, every spot, and every tissue has a special meaning. In addition to the tongue, which is the "gateway" to the interior of the body, the physician also scrutinizes the patient's fingernails and skin of his hands.

Using **hearing**, the physician listens to the patient's description of the symptoms of the disease. The patient himself knows his disease better than anyone else. In addition, the physician also listens to what the patient's family members say, as well as to the patient's breathing and coughing.

The **interview** mainly includes directing the conversation to areas that the patient did not mention himself (for example, urination and the description of the urine), as well as questions about the patient's everyday life, nutrition, work, rest, medical history, and so on.

Now comes **touch**, the most important method. The physician looks for any unusual change beneath the skin. He examines the skin temperature in different areas, skin texture, and mainly new protrusions beneath the skin.

Here, taking the patient's pulse is the most important thing. In China, this is done in the same place as in the West, on the wrist. However, it is far more important and complex in China, and serves mainly as a warning of diseases.

The Chinese physician identifies three points on the wrist: one that is similar to the point in the West, in the center of the wrist, and two others to the right and left of the center. He examines each point using two different methods: mild pressure and firm pressure. He repeats the examination on the other wrist. Thus, the physician has twelve measurements.

Every measurement can lead to one result out of about 30 possible descriptions (for instance: "like dragging a boat on a muddy slope," "like a leaf floating on the surface of a calm river"). Twelve measurements, 30 possibilities, provide a variety of tens of thousands of pulse combinations! For this reason, taking the pulse is an important means of determining the medical diagnosis.

In addition, the physician examines the patient's mental state, since the Chinese are aware of the fact that mental states such as tension or depression lead to problems in different parts of the body. Only after all the examinations have been completed does the physician, together with the patient, determine the diagnosis.

That's how it is in the East. The physician and the patient are considered a collaborating team. The physician never weighs his expertise against the patient's opinion; he always maneuvers the patient into agreeing with his diagnosis. Explanation is preferable to an unequivocal ruling! It must be remembered that as far as Chinese medicine is concerned, the patient is the one who knows the most about his condition. Why not take advantage of that knowledge?

In China, for many years, a physician would receive his fee so long as his patient was healthy. The moment the patient got ill, the physician stopped being paid. In addition, if a physician's patient died, he had to light an oil lamp at the entrance to his clinic. This is the origin of the Chinese proverb, "Stay away from a physician whose home is lit up like a palace!"

From this it is obvious why the physician tries to preserve his patients' health…

Books on Chinese medicine were written by the physicians of the Emperor and the nobles. These physicians took the trouble to expand on what was written, to elaborate upon every topic, and to go into detail… in order to safeguard their profession, of course. The more possibilities there were, the greater the detail, the harder it was for rivals to learn the entire art and jeopardize their income. However, for everyday needs, they began to devise shorter and more effective methods, similar to the structure of today's herbal handbooks.

When making a diagnosis, numerous factors must be taken into account: everything is yin or yang; external or internal; hot or cold; active or passive.

In addition, every disease invades from outside the body, makes its way via the meridians to a particular organ, and damages it. In this way, it can be cold outside and hot inside, passive outside and active inside, and so on.

There are fields of the disease: the list includes wind fields, cold fields, heat fields, wet fields, dry fields, and fire fields. In order to find the correct treatment, the physician must know the exact cause of the disease.

The physician must come up with the exact diagnosis in order to know at which specialized point he must insert the acupuncture needle or perform the massage.

Fortunately for the physicians, along with the unbearably heavy medical textbooks, they also receive a "summary."

Let's briefly survey the "summary" of Chinese medicine.

The law of the five elements states that there are five elements: wood, fire, earth, metal, and water. The body's organs are divided according to the elements, and in each element there is a yin and a yang organ, with the meridians also being divided among the five elements.

For instance, if wood contains a yin "liver," the chi network leading to the liver is wood.

The five elements are arranged in a circle that surrounds the five-pointed star, as seen.

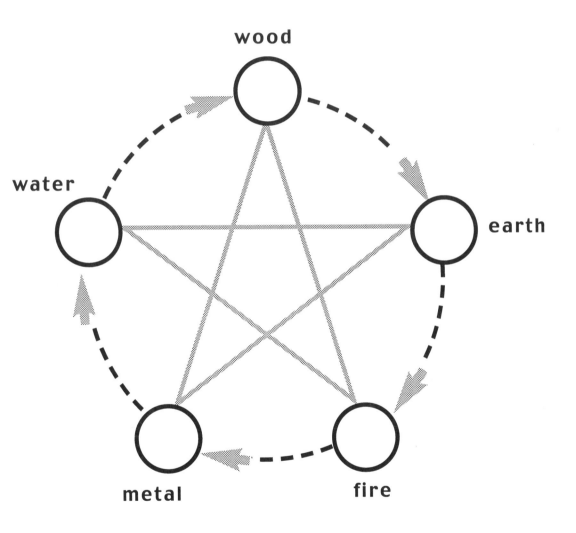

The mother-son law determines the link between the elements, and therefore it is possible to influence one chi network by treating the preceding one (the mother) or the succeeding one (the son).

The law of conquest states that one element can conquer another element, according to the direction of the arrows in the following diagram. The physician can treat one chi network in order to solve a problem in another. Here we have to remember that:

fire conquers metal by cutting it;
metal conquers wood by chopping it;
wood conquers earth by covering it;
earth conquers water by damming it;
water conquers fire by extinguishing it.

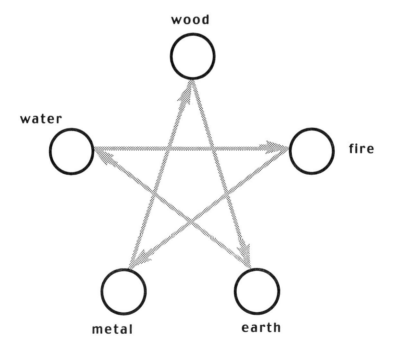

The husband-wife law relates to taking the pulse in both wrists. The right pulse is the "husband," while the left is the "wife." The husband is supposed to control the wife, while the wife contributes to stability. The physician must balance the patient so that his pulse expresses this rule.

The **noon-midnight law** states that every one of a dozen pulse measurements represents one part of a dozen body organs, and the pulse strengthens or weakens according to the time of day. Each organ has two hours a day (one of the twelve parts of the day), during which the pulse is stronger – and the peak occurs in the middle of the two hours. On the other side, that is, the dozen hours after the peak, comes the moment in which the organ has its weakest pulse. The physician must be aware of the exact time of day in which he performs the examination, and calculate the strength of the pulse of every organ.

In addition to these laws, there are detailed maps of the acupuncture regions, of the points shared by various meridians, of the intersecting, meeting, beginning and end points of every meridian.

Many theories were developed on the basis of general medicine. In acupuncture, for instance, there are methods that utilize only the small area between the base of the thumb and the index finger, finding sufficient acupuncture points in that area to cure every disease in the body. There are people who only use the ears, the feet, and so on.

It is important to understand the basis of the method of Chinese medicine. Again, remember that as much as the actions may seem strange, incomprehensible, or weird to Western eyes, every single rule in the book of Chinese medicine, every acupuncture point or massage, was checked hundreds of thousands of times prior to being set down in its final form. And if there is a method that has been tested over and over again, for thousands of years, and has achieved the desired results… why not make use of it for ourselves?

Acupuncture, acupressure, massage

The main means employed by the Chinese physician is the system of invisible networks called meridians. The meridians follow fixed paths in the body. Chi, which is the life force, the energy, flows through these networks. Chi is the invisible essence that cannot be subjected to "laboratory" tests.

There are "points" along the meridians, certain places that are each linked to a certain part of the body. When there is an upset in the yin-yang balance in a particular part of the body – in the liver, for instance – the Chinese physician believes that the upset stems from a blockage in the chi or energy flow in the networks. Acupuncture or contact with that point releases the blockage and restores the healthy balance.

The general public is familiar with terms such as acupuncture, acupressure (deep massage), shiatsu, reflexology, Swedish massage, Chinese massage. All these names are in fact different offshoots of the same theory.

Let's try to understand the principles of the overall method, the advantages and disadvantages of the components of the method (acupuncture, massage, pressure), and then we can examine, understand, and contrast the various methods.

As we mentioned previously, acupuncture originated in the Chinese army. At a certain point, someone had the idea of trying to cure his cough by sticking an arrow into his foot! And the physicians tried this – and succeeded. Over a lengthy process of experimentation, in which the whole of China was used, a method of healing was developed and documented, known today by the name "acupuncture." In order to heal and restore balance to a certain health problem, the person must be pierced at a particular point.

As early as thousands of years ago, there were thick books explaining how to diagnose the disease or the "imbalance" from which the person was suffering, and where exactly to pierce him in order to restore balance and to heal. Initially, 365 acupuncture points were marked, each of which was located on one of the meridians. Today over 1,000 acupuncture points are known.

Acupuncture was first performed with a small arrow that gradually became smaller until it turned into a thin needle, often made out of an expensive metal (even though wooden, bone or ivory needles are also used). For each treatment, the physician sticks several needles into a certain point or points for a particular length of time and at a certain depth – everything according to the diagnosis of the "imbalance."

These piercings release the blockages in the chi or energy networks and restore the yin/yang balance to the body – exactly as we join two electrical wires when we want to repair a short circuit. We cannot see the chi network or the chi itself even if we use the best scientific equipment. However, the fact remains: the method works.

There is a serious problem in the use of acupuncture in China. We know that in ancient China, operations were not performed on people as a matter of principle (nor were autopsies performed on corpses for purposes of learning), and the amputation of organs was prohibited. A Chinese person must be buried with all of his organs intact! Moreover, Chinese tradition, in many cases, does not even permit a physician to place his hand on the patient's body. In order to treat the person, the Chinese physician has to "get into the patient's skin" from a philosophical point of view. The ancient manuals teach the physician to merge, to think like the patient, to feel "as if your soul is entering his soul, as if you are living in his skin." Acupuncture, from both the physical and philosophical points of view, is a penetration into the body, a crude and focused physical invasion into the patient's body – in contradiction of all the tradition, both philosophical and medical, of ancient China.

This enables us to understand two things: first, why the treatment is administered with a very thin needle (minimal invasion of the body), and to a minimal depth within the body; second, why the Chinese sought a method to replace acupuncture, which penetrated the body, without losing the advantages afforded by acupuncture.

This method, which replaces acupuncture, or complements it, is the pressure method, which is recommended in this book mainly for self-treatment.

Pressure, whose principles are identical to those of acupuncture, means exerting pressure on a certain point in order to release a blockage and permit a free, good flow of chi. In general, this pressure is performed mainly by the thumbs, but it is possible to exert pressure with the fingertips, joints, heel of the hand, heel of the foot, special implements made for the purpose, or similar implements that create a similar effect (such as the eraser at the end of a pencil, which is widely used in acupressure). Legend has it that the pressure method, acupressure, began as a result of a lack of needles, and physicians began to use their fingernails for "acupuncture without penetration." That aside, acupressure is a widespread and effective method that appears in different forms throughout the world.

The advantages of this method lie firstly in the fact that it does not penetrate the body, and is therefore unlikely to cause an infection or an injury. In addition, the pressure is exerted on a point that is bigger than an acupuncture point, which eliminates the risk of missing the exact acupuncture point – such a risk does exist in acupuncture.

Pressure can be administered by a practitioner or a physician – but also by the patient himself, and that is an additional advantage.

The pressure methods are divided according to two main classifications: the pressure method and the location of the pressure. The Japanese ami-ma method, for example, is a series of light or hard blows that are administered like karate chops along particular areas; reflexology of the foot or of the palm of the hand is also a method of pressure on a particular area of the body; shiatsu is a pressure method on defined points along the body.

The methods are different, but the principle is identical: pressure causes the stimulation of a particular point, of a particular area, and this stimulation, through the activity of the networks, the chi, and the yin/yang balance, cures the patient.

Now we ask ourselves: How can we preempt disease, or in this case, preempt a blockage with pressure or with a blow? Perhaps there is a method to release blockages in the chi network in advance, after or before their occurrence, and preserve good health for a long time?

Acupuncture– will we pierce our bodies every day in order to prevent diseases? No way. Pressure? There is some logic here. We can probe the surface of our bodies and press on hard points that hint at a blockage. But this is still not the perfect treatment.

In order to achieve the perfect treatment, methods of healing massage were developed, a combination of massage for its own sake (a pleasurable massage) and pressures (for healing). This healing massage is a healing method that is administered easily and harmlessly. It can also be used for maintaining health, physical balance, and not only for restoring normal balance after a disruption.

Healing massage is known by many names, and all the names actually relate to the same method – medical massage, holistic massage, Chinese, Thai, or Swedish massage, and so on. We will call the various massage methods "healing massage" or "massage" for short.

Healing massage can be administered by a practitioner (not necessarily a physician), a family member, or by the patient himself (self-massage). It can be performed all over the body or on certain parts of the body (sole of foot, palm of the hand, spine, neck, and so on). It can be performed on its own or in combination with other healing methods such as acupressure and acupuncture.

Healing massage has many advantages. One is that the massage is pleasant and harmless. Also, as it is obviously relaxing, it calms the person and sends positive energy flowing through his body. Another advantage is that there is no need to pinpoint a particular disease or injury in the body – regular healing massage of the entire body once or twice a week can prevent ailments and diseases and can improve health, both spiritual and mental. Thus, the body's energetic balance is maintained.

Obviously, healing massage requires vast knowledge, but it is not knowledge that is difficult to acquire and a person can learn to administer this massage easily. Clearly, a massage that is administered by a person with whom one has a loving spiritual relationship is far more effective than one that is administered by a stranger.

Some types of healing massage concentrate on certain body systems – the flow of blood and lymph, the joints, the muscles, and so on. Other methods focus on parts of the body – the foot, the hand, the shoulders, the neck or the face. There are methods that concentrate mainly on the physical expression of the massage, such as Swedish massage, and there are methods that combine a physical massage with a "spiritual" massage. Of course, the methods also differ from one another in the depth of the massage – which ranges from vigorous rubbing to a gentle stroke, in the part of the body being massaged – the hand, fingers, feet – and in the implements that are used for the massage.

However, all the massage methods have one objective: to improve the chi or energy flow in the meridians in the human body.

The fact that these methods actually work, both in China and the West, is well known. However, we do not know exactly how and why they work. It is clear that outside intervention affects a fixed system in the human body and causes changes in its energy flow.

Researchers have attempted to understand what exactly these treatment methods affect. Some claim that it is a method of nervous stimulation which creates chemical reactions in the body. Others claim that it is a system of electrical signals that we "turn on and off" by means of the pressures.

Another approach speaks of liquids that are released during the application of pressure or the acupuncture. These liquids flow or spread through the body, in a fixed system, and repair whatever is in need of repair. These liquids can be lymphatic, acids, hormone-bearing, or endorphines that are released in the brain as a result of the pressures. These explanations are widespread mainly in the West.

In the East, especially in China, the explanation is extremely simple: chi, or energy, flows in the fixed system, and has a yin/yang balance that must be maintained.

When we want to examine, learn or use the method of acupuncture, acupressure, or the various types of massage in order to treat others or ourselves, we have to understand the principles of the method in order to make the best choice for the patient.

Chinese medicine is based on the power of chi (or ki, as it is known in Japan). The chi is the "energy steam engine," and it reflects the energy or power that creates the "steam". It is an invisible, non-measurable force – we can see and diagnose its effects, but not the force itself.

Chinese medicine finds different currents or types of energy in the body. Some of the energies are general, and are defined according to their nature – hot, cold, and so on. Others are characterized according to the particular parts of the body to which they are linked.

The energy flows along special channels – meridians. Chinese medicine distinguishes 14 main meridians: 10 that are linked to particular organs and systems; two (the triple heater and the pericardium) that are linked to physical activity: the triple heater meridian is linked mainly to reproductive power and sexuality, and the pericardial meridian is linked mainly to blood circulation; and two additional meridians, the governing meridian and the conception or central meridian, which actually balance the energies in the entire body.

Along the meridians there are various points that are linked to particular parts of the body and to diseases – to an imbalance in the body. These points are marked with letters (which symbolize the meridian) and with a number that indicates the location of the point. It is important to note that the different methods of Chinese medicine allocate different numbers to the points (even though the location remains identical). For instance, on the lung meridian in Japan, the first point is on the thumb, and the last point is on the shoulder. Note the various numberings when using different sources.

When we identify a certain point, we can use it to treat a particular imbalance (that is, disease) in the body. Some of the points are primary points – that is, we use them to administer most of the treatment – and others are secondary, and are used only by Chinese specialists.

The use of the points is for both acupuncture and massage/self-massage – the latter is recommended here. We recommend the massage of the point as a means of restoring balance in the body. This massage is performed with the tip of the thumb or with the fingertips, and the amount of pressure is determined by the masseur according to the patient's reaction. When it is a self-massage, the patient should match the depth of the massage to his own needs.

The effects of the imbalance that each primary point of a meridian treats are presented. The secondary points are not presented in detail. Each of the 14 meridians is accompanied by detailed diagrams which make the identification of the point in the body easy.

In the diagrams (for each separate meridian), there is an original Chinese diagram of the meridian, a diagram that presents the location of the meridian in the body (including the direction of the flow), and a schematic diagram of the points. In the latter, there are sometimes points that are marked with an X: these are the points that are used mainly in Japan, and they include the properties of the points next to them. Similarly, the points of the nearby meridians that "combine" with the meridian under discussion have been marked (a number combined with the letters of the meridian).

In the second part of the book, there is a detailed list of imbalances (diseases) and the primary points for treating them.

Self-treatment with meridians can be administered in two ways:
1. When there are pains or feelings of discomfort in a particular part of the body, the location of the pain must be identified by touch, and treated with a gentle massage that

gradually and cautiously becomes stronger. During the massage, the particular point or points must be reached and focused on.

2. When the disease or discomfort can be identified, it is possible to locate the points that require massage, and treat them. This is, of course, the preferred option.

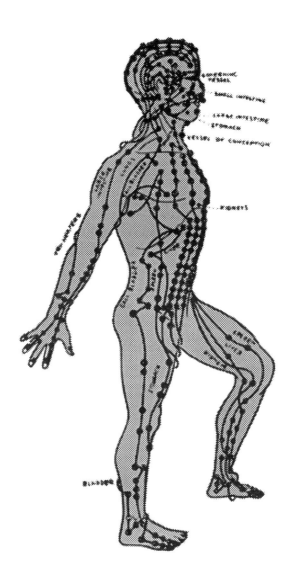

The meridians

In every sub-section:

The first diagram is an original Chinese drawing of the meridian.

The second diagram shows the location of the meridian in the body and the general directions of the flow.

The third diagram shows the meridian and the points on it.

Note that sometimes points of other meridians also appear in this diagram.

The mark X indicates a middle point that is used mainly in Japan and unites the power of the points around it.

It is important to remember:

The first 12 meridians appear in parallel on both sides of the body — the left and the right – so that there are actually two lung meridians, two large intestine meridians, and so on.

Only the two last meridians, the governing and the central meridians, are unique, because they are actually a reflection of each other.

In the diagrams, the first 12 meridians sometimes appear on the left side and sometimes on the right side of the body.

The lung meridian

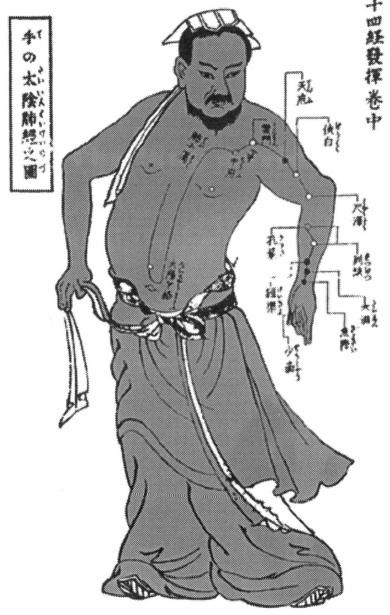

An original Chinese drawing

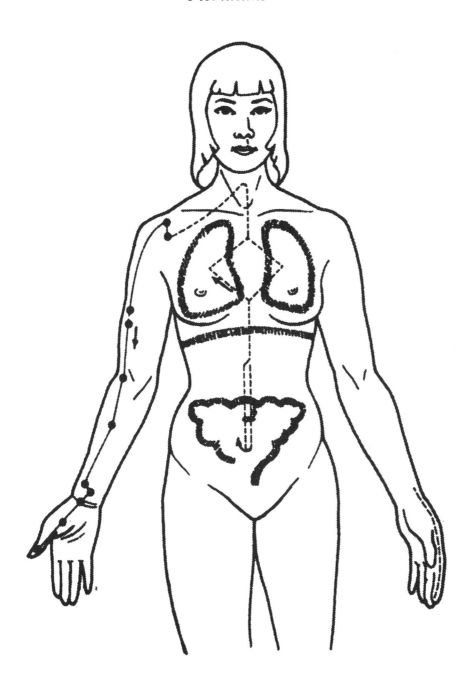

The location of the meridian

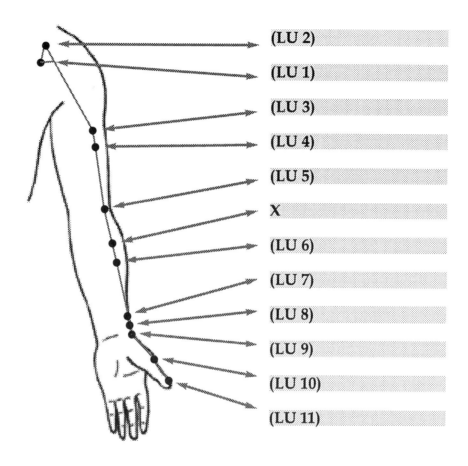

(LU 2)

(LU 1)

(LU 3)

(LU 4)

(LU 5)

X

(LU 6)

(LU 7)

(LU 8)

(LU 9)

(LU 10)

(LU 11)

The meridian and the points on it

The lung meridian
LU (P)

LU 1 -

This point relates to premature balding, balding, weakness in the heart muscle, asthma, bronchitis, a high level of acidity, pneumonia, breathing difficulties during effort.

LU 2 -

This point relates to anemia, a shortage of vitamin E, tingling of the hand.

LU 3 -

This point does not serve as a primary point.

LU 4 -

This point does not serve as a primary point.

LU 5 -

This point relates to pains in the inner part of the elbow, muscle weakness, arrhythmia, asthma, bronchitis, premature balding, mood swings, coughing, coughing blood, and sore throat.

LU 6 -

This point relates to arthritis (in the hand), coughing, coughing blood, acute asthma attacks, pain in the arms, pains in the elbow.

LU 7 -

This point relates to headaches, stiff neck, coughing, asthma, weakness in the wrist.

LU 8 -

This point does not serve as a primary point.

LU 9 –

This point relates to swelling in the lymphatic system, mood swings, blood circulation problems, asthma, bronchitis, arthritis (in the hand), coughing, forearm fracture, tonal loss in the blood vessels.

LU 10 –

This point relates to weakness in the heart muscle, arrhythmia.

LU 11 –

This point relates to a lack of energy, weakness, muscle weakness.

The large intestine meridian

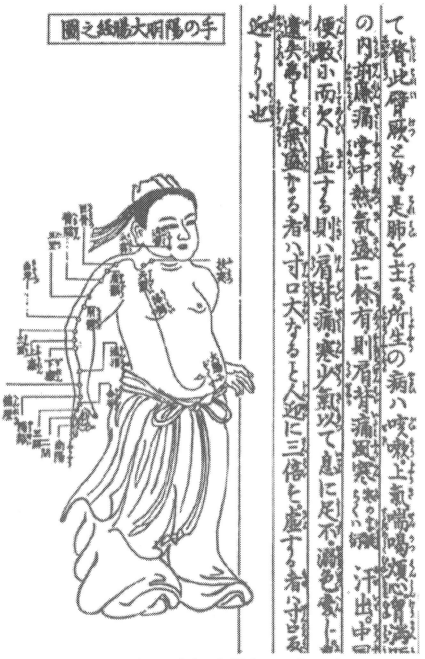

An original Chinese drawing

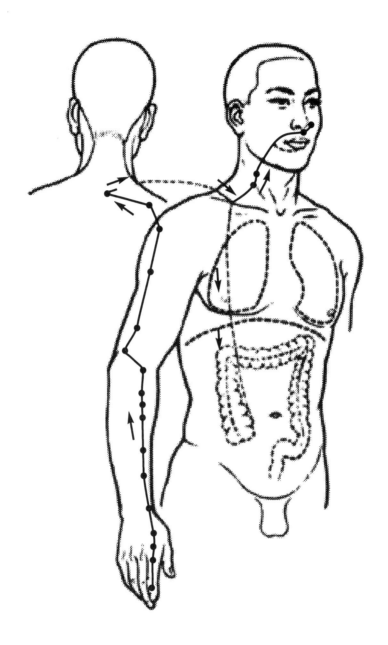

The location of the meridian

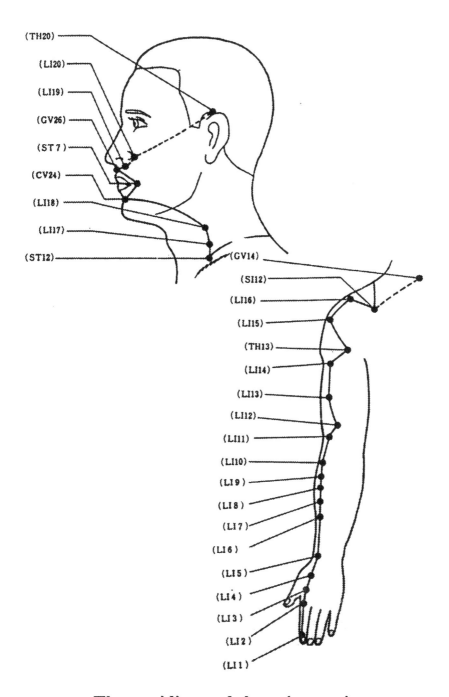

(TH20)
(LI20)
(LI19)
(GV26)
(ST 7)
(CV24)
(LI18)
(LI17)
(ST12)
(GV14)
(SI12)
(LI16)
(LI15)
(TH13)
(LI14)
(LI13)
(LI12)
(LI11)
(LI10)
(LI9)
(LI8)
(LI7)
(LI6)
(LI5)
(LI4)
(LI3)
(LI2)
(LI1)

The meridian and the points on it

The large intestine meridian
LI (GI, DI)

LI 1 –

This point relates to bedlamism.

LI 2 –

This point relates to insomnia.

LI 3 –

This point does not serve as a primary point.

LI 4 –

This point relates to miscarriage, weakness in the heart muscle, migraine, muscle weakness, headaches – mainly frontal ones, anemia, a shortage of vitamin E, inflammation of the lymph glands, facial swelling, toothaches, arrhythmia, hearing difficulties, slow pulse rate, delay of menses, arthritis of the wrist, arm fracture, sore throat, insomnia, scabies, migraine, diseases with fever without sweating.

LI 5 –

This point does not serve as a primary point.

LI 6 –

This point relates to pain in the arms, edema, hearing difficulties, nosebleeds.

LI 7 –

This point relates to shoulder and arm pains, headaches, sore throats, abdominal pains, facial swelling.

LI 8 –

This point does not serve as a primary point.

LI 9 –

This point does not serve as a primary point.

LI 10 –

This point relates to "tennis elbow".

LI 11 –
This point relates to allergies, muscle weakness, problems in the digestive system (constipation), vomiting, diarrhea, asthma, bronchitis, high or low blood pressure, fracture of the arm, "tennis elbow," diseases with fever, sore throats, muscle flaccidity, cramping, inflammation of the eyelid, colitis.

LI 12 –
This point does not serve as a primary point.

LI 13 –
This point does not serve as a primary point.

LI 14 –
This point relates to scabies.

LI 15 –
This point relates to arthritis in the hands, pain in the arms, dislocation of the shoulder, inflammation of the foot joint, pain in the shoulder blades.

LI 16 –
This point does not serve as a primary point.

LI 17 –
This point relates to inflammation.

LI 18 –
This point relates to acne vulgaris.

LI 19 –
This point does not serve as a primary point.

LI 20 –
This point relates to acne vulgaris, airsickness, anal flaccidity, runny and blocked nose, facial swelling, crookedness in the mouth.

The stomach meridian

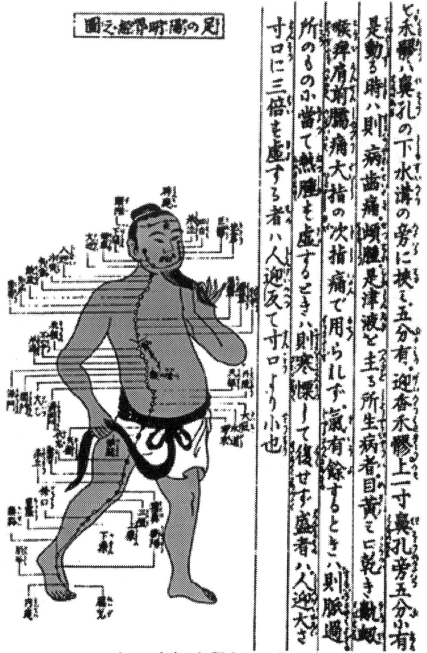

An original Chinese drawing

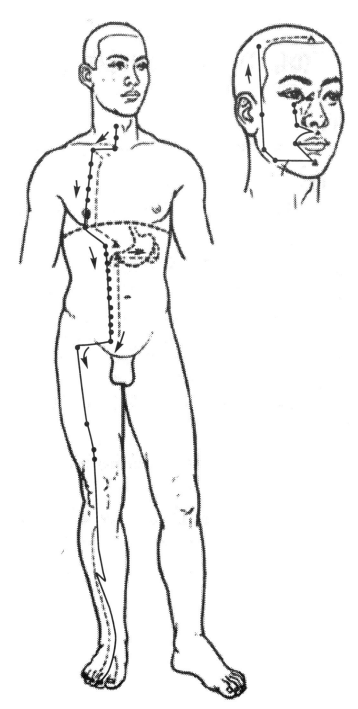

The location of the meridian

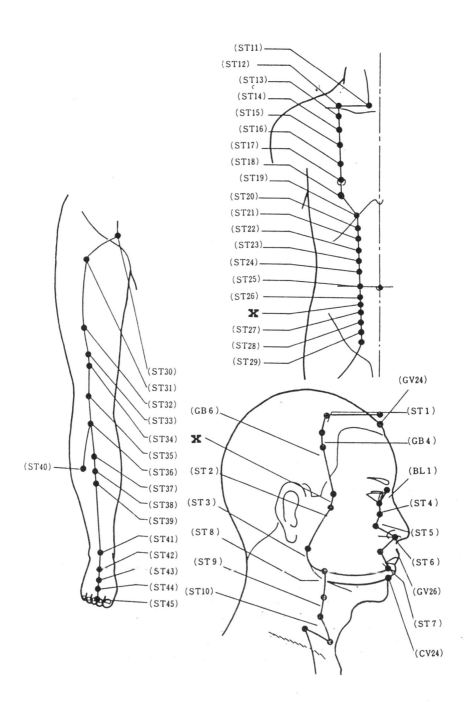

(ST11)
(ST12)
(ST13)
(ST14)
(ST15)
(ST16)
(ST17)
(ST18)
(ST19)
(ST20)
(ST21)
(ST22)
(ST23)
(ST24)
(ST25)
(ST26)
X
(ST27)
(ST28)
(ST29)

(ST30)
(ST31)
(ST32)
(ST33)
(ST34)
(ST35)
(ST36)
(ST37)
(ST38)
(ST39)
(ST41)
(ST42)
(ST43)
(ST44)
(ST45)

(ST40)

(GB6)
X
(ST2)
(ST3)
(ST8)
(ST9)
(ST10)

(GV24)
(ST1)
(GB4)
(BL1)
(ST4)
(ST5)
(ST6)
(GV26)
(ST7)
(CV24)

The meridian and the points on it

The stomach meridian
ST (M, E)

ST 1 -

This point does not serve as a primary point.

ST 2 -

This point relates to pain in the tooth socket, weakness of the eyes.

ST 3 -

This point relates to an episode of acute hemorrhoids, a tic in the eyelid, toothache, nasal congestion, swelling in the lips and cheeks.

ST 4 -

This point relates to acne vulgaris.

ST 5 -

This point relates to acne vulgaris and inflammation of the throat.

ST 6 -

This point does not serve as a primary point.

ST 7 -

This point relates to toothaches, a motor defect in the jaw, hearing difficulties, tinnitus.

ST 8 -

This point relates to acne vulgaris, congenital absence of all or part of the brain.

ST 9 -

This point relates to congenital absence of all or part of the brain, aperistalsis.

ST 10 -

This point does not serve as a primary point.

ST 11 –

This point relates to acne vulgaris, bronchial asthma.

ST 12 –

This point relates to bronchial asthma, dislocation of the shoulder.

ST 13 –

This point relates to alcoholism.

ST 14 –

This point relates to bronchial asthma, dislocation of the shoulder, pain in the bones.

ST 15 –

This point relates to lack of lactation, bronchial asthma, coughing, disease of the breast.

ST 16 –

This point does not serve as a primary point.

ST 17 –

This point relates to pain in the breast.

ST 18 –

This point does not serve as a primary point.

ST 19 –

This point relates to an inability to produce red blood cells, fluids in the abdomen following a liver disease, acidity in the stomach.

ST 20 –

This point relates to non-secretion of saliva.

ST 21 –

This point relates to abdominal pains, inflammation of the gall ducts, colitis, gastritis.

ST 22 –

This point does not serve as a primary point.

ST 23 –

This point relates to inflammation of the gall ducts, blockage of the gall ducts.

ST 24 –

This point relates to hiccups/belching.

ST 25 –

This point relates to poisoning from eating meat, abdominal pains, diarrhea, constipation, obesity, irregular menses, edema.

ST 26 –

This point relates to abdominal pains, fluids in the abdomen following a liver disease, diarrhea, gallstones, frigidity, inflammation of the abdominal muscles, flatulence in the intestines.

ST 27 –

This point relates to constipation, cramping.

ST 28 –

This point relates to alcoholism, blockage of the gall ducts.

ST 29 –

This point relates to hiccups/belching.

ST 30 –

This point relates to fluids in the abdomen following a liver disease, flatulence in the intestines, lack of menstruation, inguinal hernia, irregular menses, pains and swelling in the external reproductive organs.

ST 31 –

This point relates to pain in the thigh.

ST 32 –

This point does not serve as a primary point.

ST 33 –

This point relates to aperistalsis, cramps in the leg muscles, knee joint bursitis, pain in the thigh.

ST 34 –

This point relates to an obsession with cleanliness, cramping, back pains, abdominal pains, constipation, fracture of the lower leg.

ST 35 –

This point does not serve as a primary point.

ST 36 –

This point relates to weak muscle tone (an inability to walk), paralysis of the solar plexus, drop in energy, an obsession with cleanliness, abnormally low temperature in the limbs, airsickness, severe vomiting, inflammation of the lymph glands, inflammation of the gall ducts, aperistalsis, mood swings, pain in the ovaries, muscle weakness, fracture of the lower leg, diabetes mellitus, cramps in the leg muscles, non-secretion of saliva, atherosclerosis, abdominal pains, loss of consciousness, radiating pain, knee joint bursitis.

ST 37 –

This point relates to knee pain, partial paralysis, "tennis elbow", abdominal pains, diarrhea, menopausal phenomena.

ST 38 –

This point relates to pain in the arms.

ST 39 –

This point relates to pains in the lower abdomen, back pains, muscle degeneration, weak muscle tone (an inability to walk), motor weakness.

ST 40 –

This points relates to a lack of blood (as a result of a lack of iron), chest pains, bronchial asthma, sore throats, phlegm, muscle degeneration, motor weakness, weak muscle tone (an inability to walk), headaches, vertigo, epilepsy, mental disturbances.

ST 41 –

This points relates to exhaustion from illness, anemia as a result of a lack of vitamin E, aperistalsis, pain in the bones of the foot, gastritis, pain in the foot.

ST 42 –

This points relates to weak muscle tone (an inability to walk).

ST 43 –

This point does not serve as a primary point.

ST 44 –

This point relates to inflammation of the lymph glands, pain in the sebaceous glands, abdominal pains, diarrhea, diseases with fever, toothaches, nosebleeds, pain and swelling in the top of the foot.

ST 45 –

This point relates to anemia, atherosclerosis.

The spleen-pancreas meridian

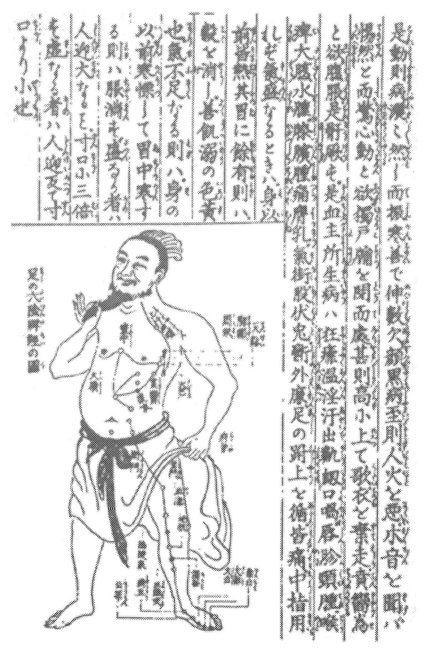

An original Chinese drawing

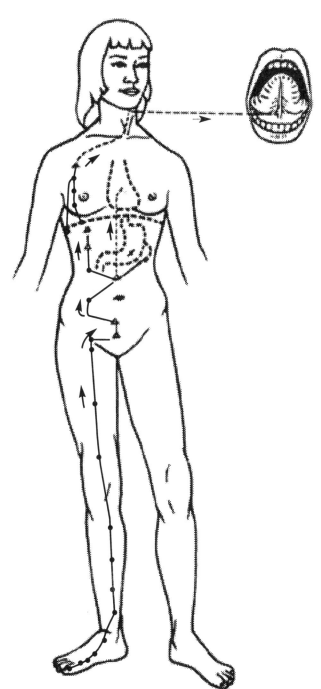

The location of the meridian

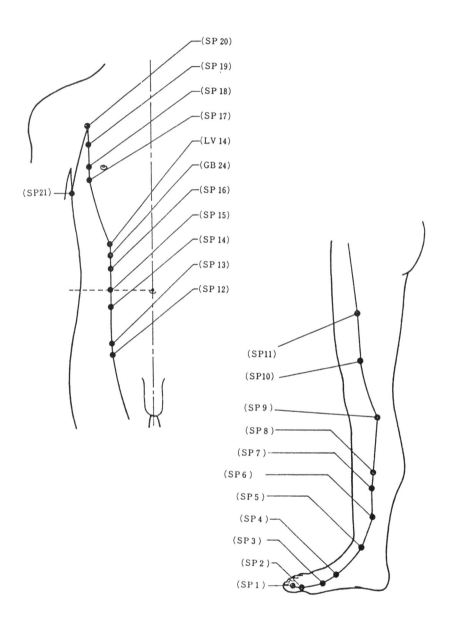

(SP 20)
(SP 19)
(SP 18)
(SP 17)
(LV 14)
(GB 24)
(SP 16)
(SP 15)
(SP 14)
(SP 13)
(SP 12)

(SP21)

(SP11)
(SP10)
(SP 9)
(SP 8)
(SP 7)
(SP 6)
(SP 5)
(SP 4)
(SP 3)
(SP 2)
(SP 1)

The meridian and the points on it

The spleen-pancreas meridian
SP (MP, RP)

SP 1 –

This point relates to anemia.

SP 2 –

This point relates to anemia as a result of a lack of iron, pain in the bones of the foot.

SP 3 –

This point relates to knock-knee, inflammation of the foot joint, abdominal pains, problems in the digestive system, vomiting, diarrhea.

SP 4 –

This point relates to weak muscle tone (an inability to walk), cramping, abdominal pains, constipation, vomiting, abdominal noises.

SP 5 –

This point relates to miscarriage, an inability to produce red blood cells, cramps in the leg muscles, hot flashes.

SP 6 –

This point relates to paralysis of the solar plexus, miscarriage, infertility, inflammation of the fallopian tubes, painful menstruation, lack of menstruation, severe vomiting, aperistalsis, non-secretion of saliva, brittle bones, blockage of the gall ducts, preliminary prolapsed uterus, vaginal discharge, cessation of menstruation, acute cystitis, scabies, tingling of the foot, a burning sensation during urination, bedwetting, flaccidity of the lower limbs, fertility problems in men and women, birth difficulties.

SP 7 –

This point relates to acne vulgaris.

SP 8 –

This point relates to pain in the ovaries, irregular menses, a burning sensation during urination, edema, severe abdominal pains.

SP 9 –

This point relates to painful menstruation, an inability to produce red blood cells, abdominal pains, diarrhea, edema, urine incontinence, knee pains, pain in the external genitalia.

SP 10 –

This point relates to skin allergies, knee joint bursitis, irregular menses, lack of menstruation, uterine bleeding, eczema, acne vulgaris.

SP 11 –

This point does not serve as a primary point.

SP 12 –

This point relates to abdominal pain, infertility, anemia as a result of a lack of iron, hemorrhoids, inflammation of the shoulder, inflammation of the ovary.

SP 13 –

This point relates to a delay of menses, inflammation of the abdominal muscles.

SP 14 –

This point relates to anemia.

SP 15 –

This point relates to poisoning from eating meat.

SP 16 –

This point relates to obesity.

SP 17 –

This point relates to aperistalsis.

SP 18 –

This point does not serve as a primary point.

SP 19 –

This point relates to anemia, inflammation of the throat, pain in the breast.

SP 20 –

This point relates to underdevelopment of the heart, coughing.

SP 21 –

This point relates to abdominal pain, infertility, disease of the breast, general itching, pains under the ribs, bronchial asthma.

The heart meridian

少陰心之経熱踏臂肘病攣狂
絡相較さる直者の如く

竹の下廉の上に居て朝之

五椎心所以を

心系心臓に心や心中心心起て

心系小腸小腸小下り小

八則肺恭う下で幽折て系むうい術骨小並無る相連也本臓を

心系二あり一八則上腸と

通に肺の而大恭の間小

通に肺の而大恭の如く

に通する 也手の少陰の恭心小起て任脈之外と術て心系小腸ー腸小下

絡の上二寸る分小常て小腸を恭ふ

An original Chinese drawing

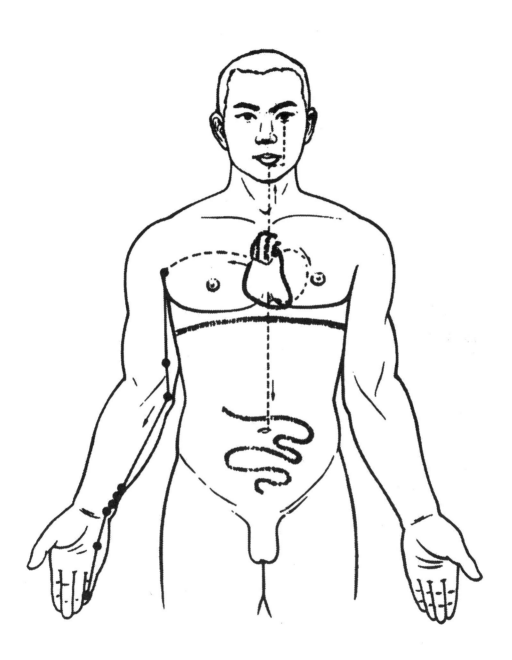

The location of the meridian

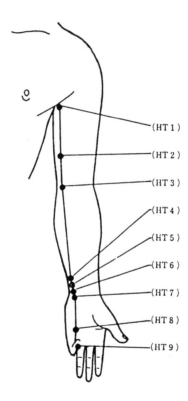

(HT 1)

(HT 2)

(HT 3)

(HT 4)

(HT 5)

(HT 6)

(HT 7)

(HT 8)

(HT 9)

The meridian and the points on it

The heart meridian
HT (C)

HT 1 –

This point relates to loss of balance, lack of lactation.

HT 2 –

This point relates to "tennis elbow."

HT 3 –

This point relates to a cessation of sensation, chest pains while reclining, chest pains, heartburn, tingling of the arm, hand tremor, "tennis elbow," Parkinson's disease.

HT 4 –

This point relates to lack of lactation, heartburn, hoarseness or sudden loss of voice, convulsions.

HT 5 –

This point relates to vertigo, an inability to write (stemming from the brain), blurred vision, pains in the wrist.

HT 6 –

This point relates to weakness in the heart muscle, inflammation of the eyelid, hysteria, night sweats.

HT 7 –

This point relates to paralysis of the solar plexus, an obsession with cleanliness, arrhythmia, constipation, fracture of the forearm, sleeping difficulties, feeling of heat in the hands, epilepsy, mental disturbances, memory lapses, mental unease.

HT 8 –

This point relates to weakness of the eyes, underdevelopment of the heart.

HT 9 –

This point relates to weakness in the heart muscle, slow heartbeat, an inability to sleep.

The small intestine meridian

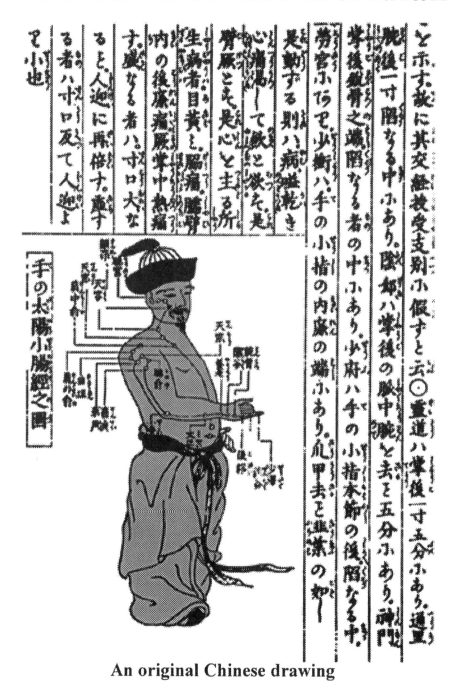

An original Chinese drawing

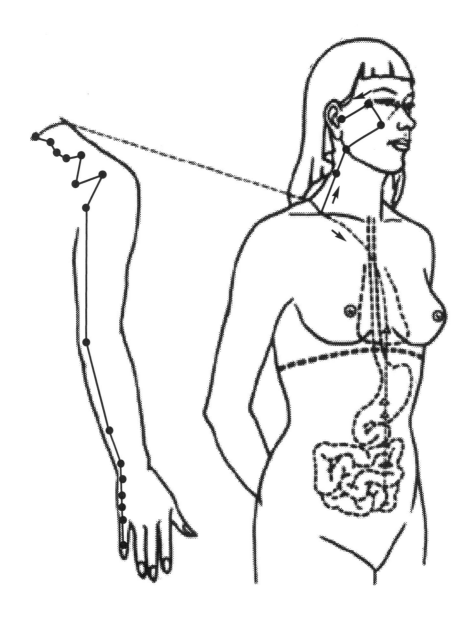

The location of the meridian

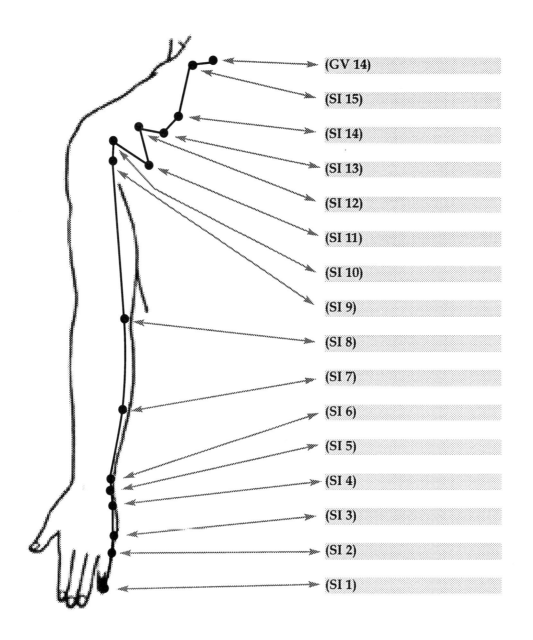

(GV 14)

(SI 15)

(SI 14)

(SI 13)

(SI 12)

(SI 11)

(SI 10)

(SI 9)

(SI 8)

(SI 7)

(SI 6)

(SI 5)

(SI 4)

(SI 3)

(SI 2)

(SI 1)

The meridian and the points on it

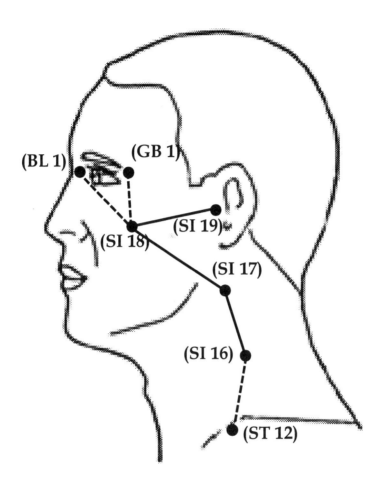

The location of the meridian

The small intestine meridian
SI (IG)

SI 1 -

This point relates to lack of lactation, tingling of the hand.

SI 2 -

This point relates to a cessation of sensation.

SI 3 -

This point relates to premature balding, congenital absence of all or part of the brain, aperistalsis, arthritis of the wrist, an inability to sleep, poisoning from eating meat, headaches, stiff neck, congestion in the eyes, hearing difficulties, diseases with fever, epilepsy, night sweats.

SI 4 -

This point relates to poisoning from eating meat, tingling of the hand, headaches, stiff neck, diseases with fever, hepatitis.

SI 5 -

This point relates to gastritis.

SI 6 -

This point relates to abdominal pains, blurred vision, pains in the shoulder, back, neck, elbow, and arm.

SI 7 -

This point relates to angina pectoris.

SI 8-

This point relates to overexcitedness, gastritis, radiating pain, pains in the nape of the neck, shoulder, and arm, epilepsy.

SI 9 -

This point relates to an inability to write (stemming from the brain).

SI 10 –
This point relates to disease of the lymph glands, an inability to sleep.

SI 11 –
This point relates to pains in the shoulders and scapulae.

SI 12 –
This point relates to inflammation of the shoulder.

SI 13 –
This point relates to pains in the shoulders and scapulae.

SI 14 –
This point relates to inflammation of the shoulder, tingling of the hand.

SI 15 –
This point relates to a neurological syndrome following a stroke, laryngitis.

SI 16 –
This point relates to pain in the shoulder blades.

SI 17 –
This point does not serve as a primary point.

SI 18 –
This point relates to acne vulgaris.

SI 19 –
This point relates to congenital absence of all or part of the brain, hearing difficulties, earaches, tinnitus, pains in the upper jaw, vertigo.

The bladder meridian

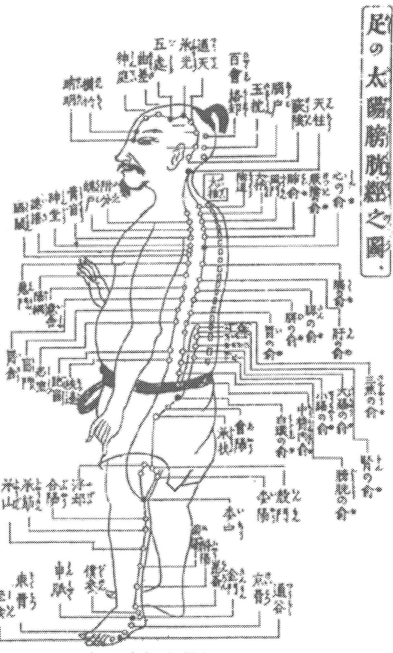

An original Chinese drawing

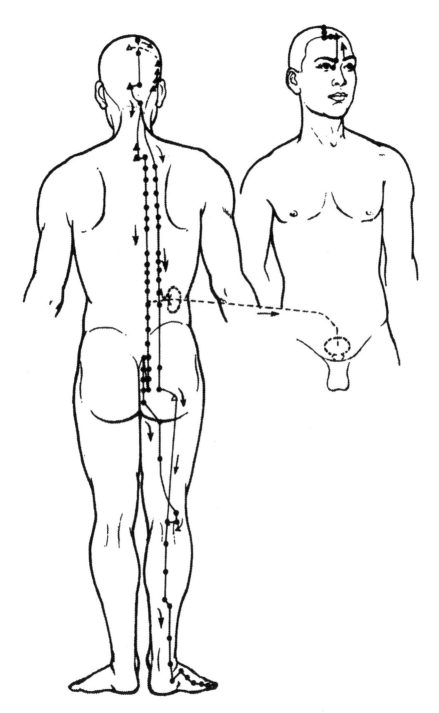

The location of the meridian

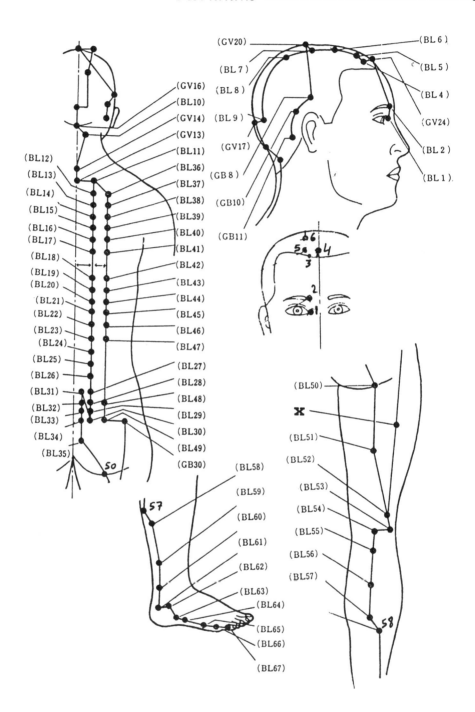

(GV20)
(BL 7)
(GV16)
(BL10)
(GV14)
(GV13)
(BL11)
(BL 8)
(BL 9)
(GV17)
(BL36)
(BL37)
(GB 8)
(BL38)
(GB10)
(BL39)
(BL40)
(GB11)
(BL41)
(BL42)
(BL43)
(BL44)
(BL45)
(BL46)
(BL47)
(BL27)
(BL28)
(BL48)
(BL29)
(BL30)
(BL49)
(GB30)

(BL12)
(BL13)
(BL14)
(BL15)
(BL16)
(BL17)
(BL18)
(BL19)
(BL20)
(BL21)
(BL22)
(BL23)
(BL24)
(BL25)
(BL26)
(BL31)
(BL32)
(BL33)
(BL34)
(BL35)

(BL 6)
(BL 5)
(BL 4)
(GV24)
(BL 2)
(BL 1)

(BL50)
(BL51)
(BL52)
(BL53)
(BL54)
(BL55)
(BL56)
(BL57)

(BL58)
(BL59)
(BL60)
(BL61)
(BL62)
(BL63)
(BL64)
(BL65)
(BL66)
(BL67)

The meridian and the points on it

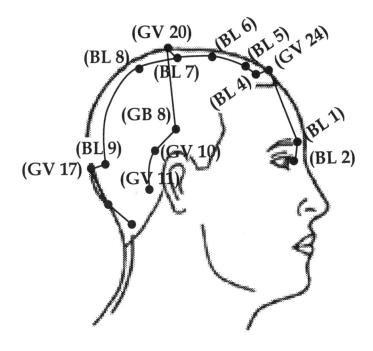

The meridian and the points on it

The bladder meridian
BL, BI (V)

BI 1 –

This point relates to pain in the tooth socket, hemorrhoid attacks, nasal dryness.

BI 2 –

This point relates to airsickness, congenital absence of all or part of the brain, functional problems as a result of a stroke, weakness of the eyes, episode of acute hemorrhoids, impotence.

BI 3 –

This point does not serve as a primary point.

BI 4 –

This point relates to airsickness, episode of acute hemorrhoids.

BI 5 –

This point relates to airsickness.

BI 6 –

This point does not serve as a primary point.

BI 7 –

This point does not serve as a primary point.

BI 8 –

This point does not serve as a primary point.

BI 9 –

This point does not serve as a primary point.

BI 10 –

This point relates to bronchial asthma, impotence.

BI 11 –

This point relates to the after-effects of head injuries, chest pains.

BI 12 –

This point relates to tingling of the hand.

BI 13 –

This point relates to diabetes mellitus.

BI 14 –

This point relates to atherosclerosis, heartburn.

BI 15 –

This point relates to chest pains, heartburn, night sweats.

BI 16 –

This point does not serve as a primary point.

BI 17 –

This point relates to an obsession with cleanliness.

BI 18 –

This point relates to inflammation of the fallopian tubes.

BI 19 –

This point does not serve as a primary point.

BI 20 –

This point relates to pains with a neurological source, diabetes mellitus.

BI 21 –

This point relates to disease of the lymph glands, colitis.

BI 22 –

This point does not serve as a primary point.

Bl 23 -

This point relates to stoppage of urine, diabetes mellitus, impotence, kidney pains.

Bl 24 -

This point relates to hemorrhoids.

Bl 25 -

This point relates to fluids in the abdomen following a liver disease, hemorrhoids, inflammation of the uterus lining.

Bl 26 -

This point relates to a fracture of the coccyx.

Bl 27 -

This point relates to menstrual pains, cessation of menstruation.

Bl 28 -

This point relates to stoppage of urine, massive internal bleeding (a stroke), bedwetting, inflammation of the uterus lining, tingling of the foot.

Bl 29 -

This point relates to hemorrhoids, impotence, sciatica.

Bl 30 -

This point relates to low sperm (quantity or quality).

Bl 31 -

This point relates to weak muscle tone (an inability to walk), inflammation of the fallopian tubes, fracture of the coccyx.

Bl 32 -

This point relates to weak muscle tone (an inability to walk), menstrual pains, stoppage of urine, acute cystitis, impotence, lumbago.

BI 33 –

This point relates to cessation of menstruation, acute cystitis, anal itching.

BI 34 –

This point relates to menstrual pains, stoppage of urine, fracture of the coccyx, anal itching.

BI 35 –

This point relates to inflammation of the uterus lining, lumbago.

BI 36 –

This point relates to pain in the thigh, tingling of the foot, anal itching.

BI 37 –

This point relates to sciatica.

BI 38 –

This point relates to knee joint bursitis, yellowness of the skin.

BI 39 –

This point does not serve as a primary point.

BI 40 –

This point relates to pain in the ovaries, knee joint bursitis.

BI 41-54 –

These points relate to massive bleeding (a stroke), a burning sensation in the abdomen.

BI 41-52 –

These points relate to kidney pains.

BI 41 –

This point relates to excessive sweating, tingling of the hand.

BI 42 –

This point relates to inflammation of the shoulder, tingling of the hand.

BI 45 –

This point relates to bronchial asthma, pain in the shoulder blades.

BI 49 –

This point relates to diabetes mellitus.

BI 53 –

This point relates to an inability to produce red blood cells, bedwetting.

BI 54 –

This point does not serve as a primary point.

BI 55 –

This point does not serve as a primary point.

BI 56 –

This point relates to pain in the thigh.

BI 57 –

This point relates to pain in the arms.

BI 58 –

This point relates to pain in the achilles tendon.

BI 59 –

This point relates to pain in the achilles tendon.

BI 60 –

This point relates to pain in the achilles tendon, pain in the foot, inflammation of the foot joint.

BI 61 –

This point relates to pain in the achilles tendon, an inability to produce red blood cells, prominent heel.

BI 62 –

This point does not serve as a primary point.

BI 63 –

This point relates to hearing difficulties, radiating pain, prominent heel.

BI 64 –

This point relates to inflammation of the foot joint.

BI 65 –

This point relates to acute cystitis, knee joint bursitis, poisoning from eating meat.

BI 66 –

This point does not serve as a primary point.

BI 67 –

This point relates to hot flashes.

The kidney meridian

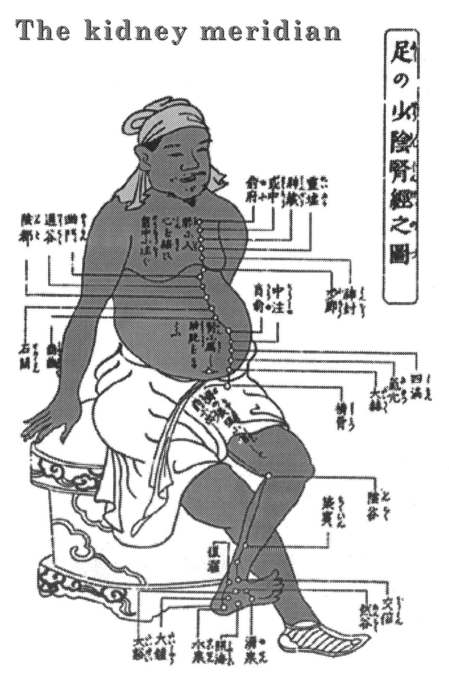

An original Chinese drawing

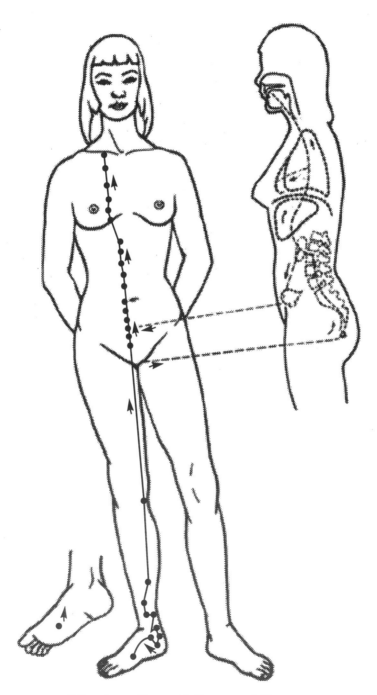

The location of the meridian

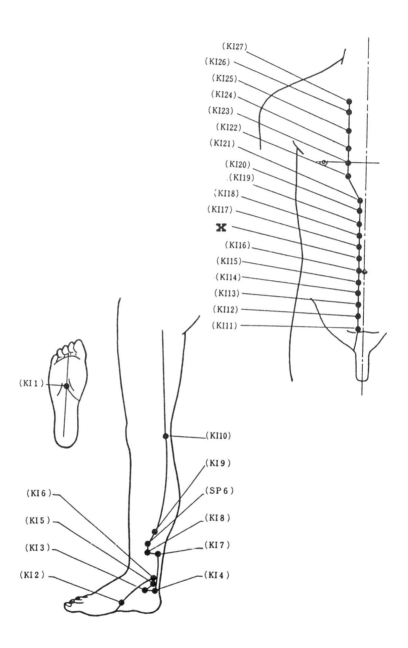

(KI27)
(KI26)
(KI25)
(KI24)
(KI23)
(KI22)
(KI21)
(KI20)
.(KI19)
(KI18)
(KI17)
X
(KI16)
(KI15)
(KI14)
(KI13)
(KI12)
(KI11)

(KI 1)

(KI10)
(KI 9)
(SP 6)
(KI 8)
(KI 7)
(KI 4)

(KI 6)
(KI 5)
(KI 3)
(KI 2)

The meridian and the points on it

The kidney meridian
K (R)

K 1 -
This point relates to diseases of the lymph glands, anemia, arrhythmia, bedwetting, urine incontinence, irritation, vertigo, infant convulsions, loss of consciousness, sore throat, blurred vision, dry tongue, loss of voice.

K 2 -
This point relates to bedwetting, weak muscle tone (an inability to walk), pain in the foot, prolapsed uterus, irregular menses, diarrhea, bloody saliva, pain and swelling in the top of the foot.

K 3 -
This point relates to sore throat, toothache, hearing difficulties, asthma, irregular menses, frequent urination, difficulties in falling asleep, lumbago.

K 4 -
This point relates to prominent heel, pain in the bones of the foot, asthma, bloody saliva, lumbar and sacral pain.

K 5 -
This point relates to pain in the heel, acute cystitis, fracture of the lower leg, pain in the ovaries, prominent heel, irregular menses, menstrual pains, prolapsed uterus, pains during urination, blurred vision.

K 6 -
This point relates to pains that stem from a neurological source, cramps in the leg muscles, the first stages of a prolapsed uterus, irregular menses, hernia in the groin, frequent urination, epilepsy, difficulties in falling asleep, sore throat, loss of voice.

K 7 –

This point relates to weak muscle tone (an inability to walk), frigidity, excessive sweating, pain in the foot, abdominal pains, diarrhea, night sweats and spontaneous sweating, edema, edema in the leg, muscle degeneration in the leg, weakness of the foot.

K 8 –

This point relates to lack of menstruation.

K 9 –

This point relates to weak muscle tone (an inability to walk), cramps in the leg muscles.

K 10 –

This point relates to underdevelopment of the heart, tonal loss in the blood vessels, pain in the ovaries, radiating pain.

K 11 –

This point relates to premature balding, fluids in the abdomen following a liver disease, excessive sweating, flatulence in the intestines, inflammation of the ovary.

K 12 –

This point relates to infertility, delay of menses, urine incontinence, hot flashes.

K 13 –

This point relates to infertility, flatulence in the intestines.

K 14 –

This point relates to inflammation of the gall ducts.

K 15 –

This point relates to disease of the lymph glands, urine incontinence, inflammation of the abdominal muscles.

K 16 –

This point relates to inflammation of the gall ducts, flatulence in the intestines.

K 17 –

This point relates to a stroke, kidney pains, general itching.

K 18 –

This point does not serve as a primary point.

K 19 –

This point does not serve as a primary point.

K 20 –

This point relates to premature balding.

K 21 –

This point relates to anemia.

K 22 –

This point does not serve as a primary point.

K 23 –

This point relates to night sweats.

K 24 –

This point relates to pain in the breast.

K 25 –

This point relates to pain in the breast.

K 26 –

This point does not serve as a primary point.

K 27 –

This point relates to premature balding, laryngitis, asthma, coughing, chest pains.

The pericardium meridian

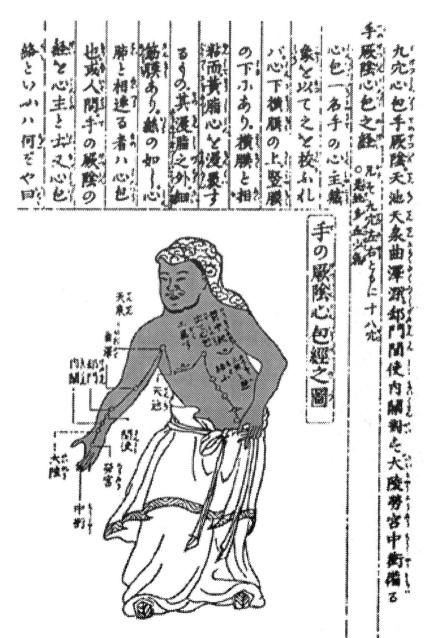

An original Chinese drawing

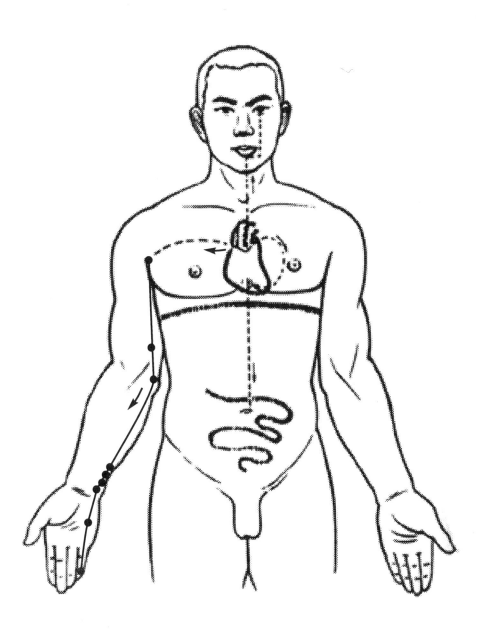

The location of the meridian

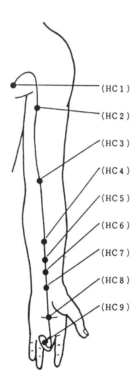

(HC 1)

(HC 2)

(HC 3)

(HC 4)

(HC 5)

(HC 6)

(HC 7)

(HC 8)

(HC 9)

The meridian and the points on it

The pericardium meridian
HC (MC)

HC 1 –

This point relates to alcoholism, dislocation of the shoulder, inflammation of the shoulder.

HC 2 –

This point relates to chest pains while reclining.

HC 3 –

This point relates to alcoholism, weakness in the heart muscle, slow heartbeat, "tennis elbow," abdominal pains, vomiting, diseases with fever, mental unease, pains in the center of the elbow, hand tremor.

HC 4 –

This point relates to migraine, "tennis elbow," boils, nosebleeds, cardiac pains.

HC 5 –

This point relates to cardiac pains, diseases with fever, vomiting, epilepsy, mental disturbances, pain in the arms.

HC 6 –

This point relates to paralysis of the solar plexus, an obsession with cleanliness, severe vomiting, chest pains while reclining, chest pains, heartburn, slow heart contractions, mental disturbances, epilepsy, diseases with fever, pain in the elbow and forearm.

HC 7 –

This point relates to arthritis of the wrist, cardiac pains, mental disturbances, vomiting, hysteria.

HC 8 –

This point relates to acute heart attack, an obsession with cleanliness, slow heart contractions, arthritis of the wrist, general itching.

HC 9 –

This point relates to tingling of the hand.

The triple heater meridian

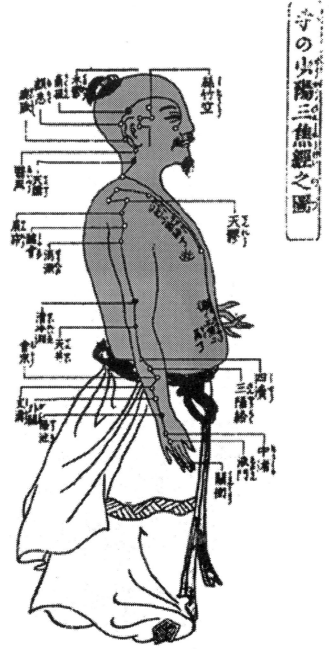

An original Chinese drawing

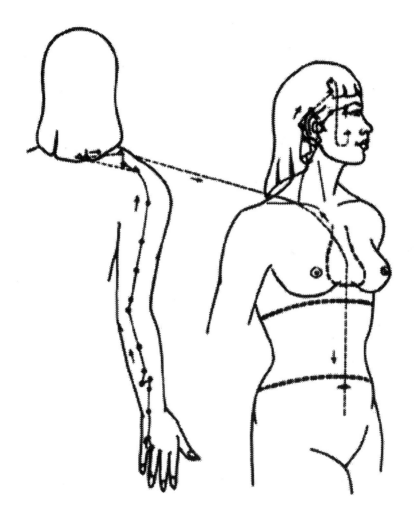

The location of the meridian

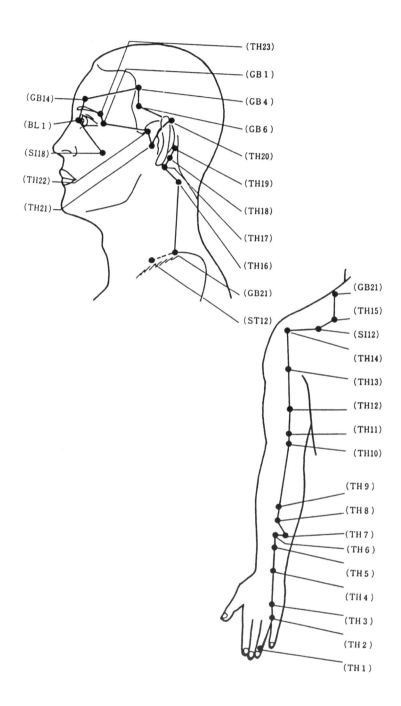

(TH23)
(GB 1)
(GB14)
(GB 4)
(BL 1)
(GB 6)
(SI18)
(TH20)
(TH22)
(TH19)
(TH21)
(TH18)
(TH17)
(TH16)
(GB21)
(ST12)
(GB21)
(TH15)
(SI12)
(TH14)
(TH13)
(TH12)
(TH11)
(TH10)
(TH 9)
(TH 8)
(TH 7)
(TH 6)
(TH 5)
(TH 4)
(TH 3)
(TH 2)
(TH 1)

The meridian and the points on it

The triple heater meridian
TW, TH (TR)

TW 1 –

This point relates to abnormally low temperature in the limbs, an inability to write (stemming from the brain).

TW 2 –

This point relates to tingling of the hand.

TW 3 –

This point relates to abnormally low temperature in the limbs, delay of menses, an inability to sleep, hypertension, headaches, hearing defects, tinnitis, diseases with fever, motor defects in the fingers.

TW 4 –

This point relates to an inability to write (stemming from the brain), general itching, pains in the joints, shoulder, and forearm, hearing defects.

TW 5 –

This point relates to disease of the lymph glands, diseases with fever, headaches, hearing defects, tinnitis, motor defects in the arm, elbow and forearm, hand tremor.

TW 6 –

This point does not serve as a primary point.

TW 7 –

This point relates to pains in the upper limbs, epilepsy, sudden deafness.

TW 8 –

This point relates to disease of the blood vessels.

TW 9 –

This point relates to abnormally low temperature in the limbs, "tennis elbow."

TW 10 –
This point relates to exhaustion from illness, slow heartbeat, slow heart contractions, lack of energy, "tennis elbow," headache on one side, pain in the ribs, pains in the neck, shoulder and hand, epilepsy.

TW 11 –
This point relates to night sweats.

TW 12 –
This point relates to "tennis elbow," hearing defects, tinnitis, swelling in the cheeks.

TW 13 –
This point relates to inflammation of the shoulder.

TW 14 –
This point relates to a drop in energy, arthritis in the shoulder, general itching, pain in the shoulder blades, night sweats.

TW 15 –
This point relates to weakness, night sweats, inflammation of the throat, a lack of self-control.

TW 16 –
This point relates to laryngitis, blockage of the gall ducts.

TW 17 –
This point relates to migraine, a lack of self-control, obesity.

TW 18 –
This point relates to hypertension.

TW 19 –
This point does not serve as a primary point.

TW 20 –

This point does not serve as a primary point.

TW 21 –

This point relates to weakness, toothache, hearing defects, ear diseases.

TW 22 –

This point relates to acne vulgaris.

TW 23 –

This point relates to acne vulgaris, inflammation of the eyelid, nasal dryness, migraine, blurred vision, pains in the eyes.

The gall bladder meridian

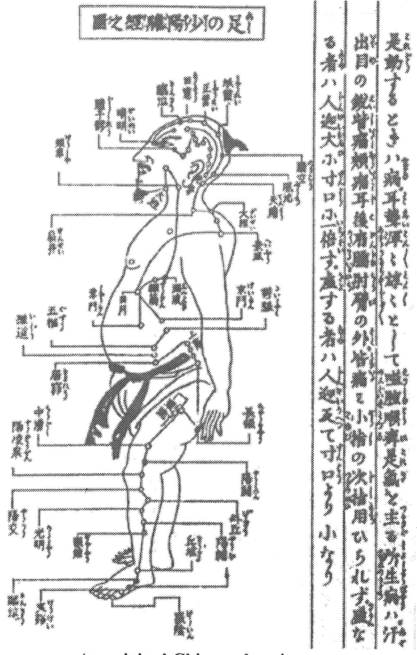

An original Chinese drawing

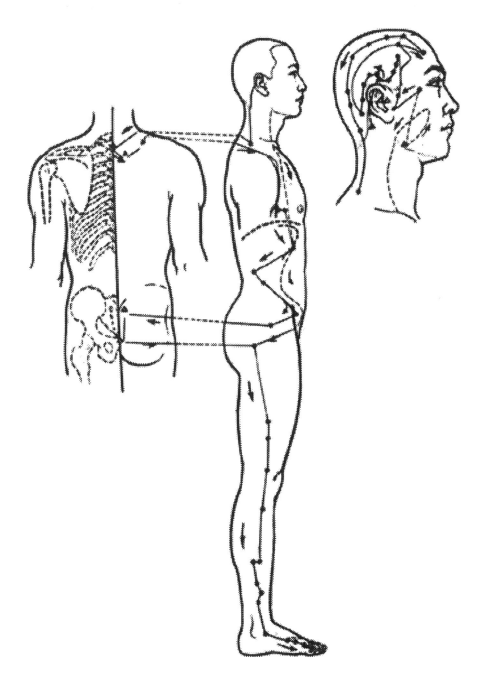

The location of the meridian

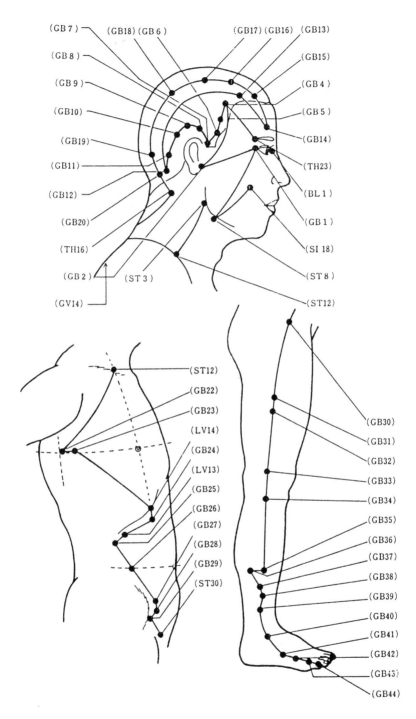

The meridian and the points on it

The gall bladder meridian
GB (VB)

GB 1 –

This point relates to weakness of the eyes, inflammation of the eyelid, nasal dryness, lateral headache, pains in the eyes, excessive watering of the eyes.

GB 2 –

This point relates to hearing difficulties, tinnitis, toothache.

GB 3 –

This point does not serve as a primary point.

GB 4 –

This point relates to airsickness.

GB 5 –

This point relates to nausea.

GB 6 –

This point does not serve as a primary point.

GB 7 –

This point does not serve as a primary point.

GB 8 –

This point relates to a neurological syndrome following a stroke, lateral headache, quitting smoking.

GB 9 –

This point does not serve as a primary point.

GB 10 –

This point does not serve as a primary point.

GB 11 –

This point relates to a lack of self-control.

GB 12 –

This point relates to congenital absence of all or part of the brain.

GB 13 –

This point does not serve as a primary point.

GB 14 –

This point relates to an anterior headache, blurred vision, excessive watering of the eyes as a result of exposure to the wind, a tic in the eyelid.

GB 15 –

This point relates to alcoholism, an anterior headache, nasal congestion, blurred vision.

GB 16 –

This point relates to airsickness.

GB 17 –

This point relates to night sweats.

GB 18 –

This point does not serve as a primary point.

GB 19 –

This point does not serve as a primary point.

GB 20 –

This point relates to alcoholism, tingling of the hand, headache, vertigo, pain and inflammation of the eyes, back and shoulder pains, diseases with fever, colds, influenza.

GB 21 –

This point relates to general itching.

GB 22 –

This point relates to inflammation of the shoulder, pain in the bones.

GB 23 –

This point relates to pain in the breast.

GB 24 –

This point relates to heartburn, vomiting, hiccups/belching.

GB 25 –

This point relates to obesity, flatulence in the intestines, diarrhea, abdominal pain, lumbago.

GB 26 –

This point relates to inflammation of the fallopian tubes, inflammation of the abdominal muscles, yellowness of the skin.

GB 27 –

This point relates to low sperm (quantity or quality), vaginal discharges, hiatus hernia, hernia in the groin, lower back and pelvis pain.

GB 28 –

This point relates to delay of menses, hiatus or inguinal hernia, lower back and pelvis pain, vaginal discharges, prolapsed uterus.

GB 29 –

This point relates to frigidity.

GB 30 –

This point relates to lower back and pelvis pain, muscle degeneration, motor weakness and pains in the lower limbs.

GB 31 –

This point does not serve as a primary point.

GB 32 –

This point relates to knock knee, pain in the thigh.

GB 33 –

This point relates to knock knee, pain in the thigh.

GB 34 –

This point relates to weak muscle tone (an inability to walk), inflammation of the fallopian tubes, knee joint bursitis, pain in the ribs, vomiting, a bitter taste in the mouth.

GB 35 –

This point does not serve as a primary point.

GB 36 –

This point relates to pains in the neck, chest, and rib region.

GB 37 –

This point relates to knee pains, motor weakness and pains in the lower limbs, muscle degeneration, pains in the eyes, night blindness, toothache.

GB 38 –

This point relates to gallstones.

GB 39 –

This point relates to gastritis, pains and fullness in the chest, pains in the rib region, pain in the thigh, knee joint bursitis.

GB 40 –

This point relates to pain in the bones of the foot, pains in the neck and chest, diseases with fever, headaches.

GB 41 –

This point relates to weak muscle tone (an inability to walk).

GB 42 –

This point relates to inflammation of the foot joint.

GB 43 –

This point relates to brittleness of the bones, pain in the bones of the foot, blockage of the gall ducts, inflammation of the foot joint, blurred vision, pains in the cheeks, pains in the lower jaw and in the ribs, diseases with fever, tinnitis.

GB 44 –

This point relates to knock-knee.

The liver meridian

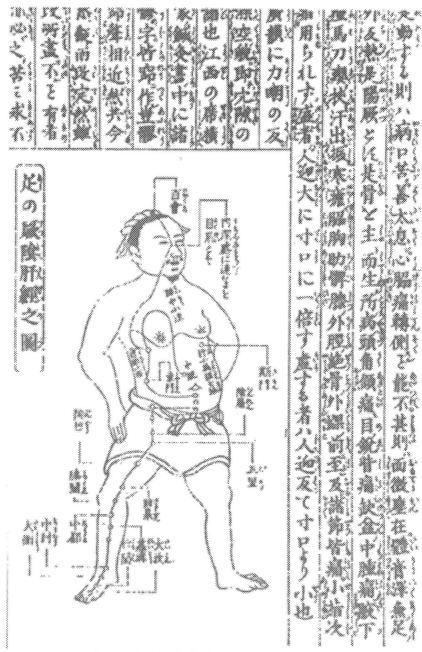

An original Chinese drawing

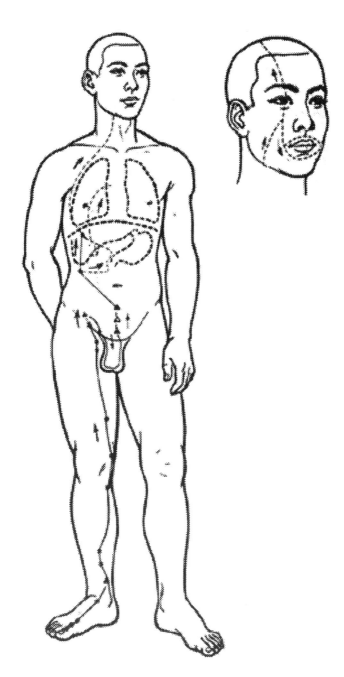

The location of the meridian

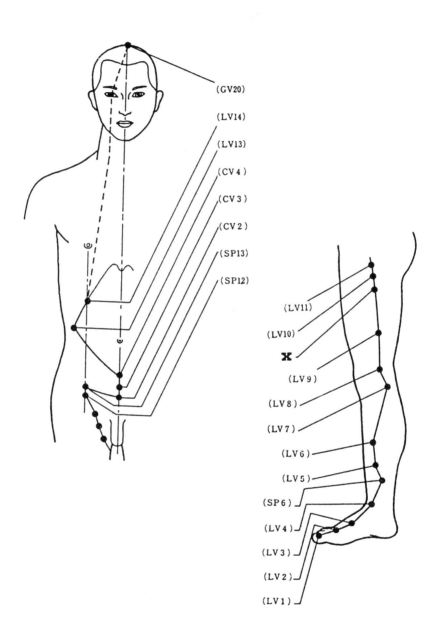

(GV20)

(LV14)

(LV13)

(CV 4)

(CV 3)

(CV 2)

(SP13)

(SP12)

(LV11)

(LV10)

x

(LV 9)

(LV 8)

(LV 7)

(LV 6)

(LV 5)

(SP 6)

(LV 4)

(LV 3)

(LV 2)

(LV 1)

The meridian and the points on it

The liver meridian
LIV (F)

LIV 1 -
This point relates to inflammation of the foot joint.

LIV 2 -
This point relates to inflammation of the gall ducts, acute cystitis, yellowness of the skin, pain in the foot, bleeding between menses, uterine pain, bedwetting, redness and swelling in the eye, pain in the rib region, headaches, blurred vision, epilepsy, difficulties in falling asleep, convulsions.

LIV 3 -
This point relates to infertility, lack of menstruation, tonal loss in the blood vessels, inflammation of the gallbladder, uterine bleeding, bedwetting, crookedness of the mouth, epilepsy, headaches, difficulties in falling asleep.

LIV 4 -
This point does not serve as a primary point.

LIV 5 -
This point relates to irregular menses, pain during urination, hernia in the groin, pains in the legs.

LIV 6 -
This point relates to hernia in the groin, uterine bleeding.

[LIV 7 -
This point relates to a fracture of the lower leg.

LIV 8 -
This point relates to infertility, inflammation of the gallbladder, cramps in the leg muscles, prolapsed uterus, menstrual pains, lower abdominal pains, pains during urination, pains in the external genitals, pains in the knee and the center of the thigh.

LIV 9 –
This point relates to acute cystitis, knock-knee.

LIV 10 –
This point relates to hernia in the groin.

LIV 11 –
This point relates to general itching.

LIV 12 –
This point relates to ascites, flatulence in the intestines.

LIV 13 –
This point relates to obesity, yellowness of the skin, digestive difficulties, abdominal pains, pains in the hips, pains beneath and between the ribs.

LIV 14 –
This point relates to gallstones, pains in the chest and the ribs, abdominal pains, vomiting, hiccups/belching.

The governing meridian

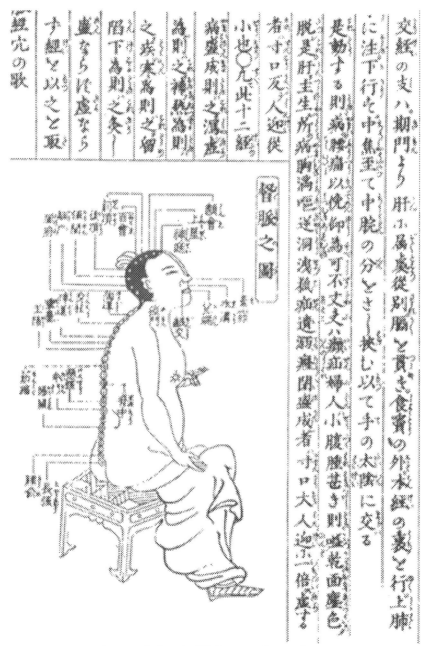

An original Chinese drawing

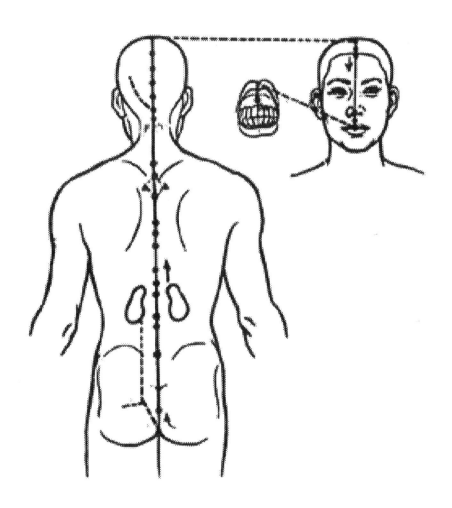

The location of the meridian

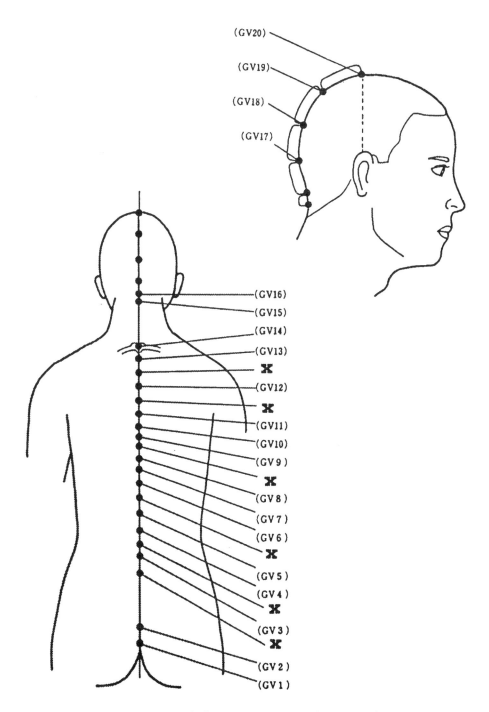

(GV20)
(GV19)
(GV18)
(GV17)

(GV16)
(GV15)
(GV14)
(GV13)
✖
(GV12)
✖
(GV11)
(GV10)
(GV 9)
✖
(GV 8)
(GV 7)
(GV 6)
✖
(GV 5)
(GV 4)
✖
(GV 3)
✖
(GV 2)
(GV 1)

The meridian and the points on it

The governing meridian
DU-GV (VG)

GV 1 -
This point relates to miscarriage, weakness, balding, anemia as a result of bleeding, disease of the blood vessels, back pains, fracture of the coccyx, hernia in the groin, sciatica, lumbago, inflammation of the uterus lining.

GV 2 -
This point relates to low sperm (quantity or quality), sciatica, lumbago, inflammation of the uterus lining, lower back and pelvis pain.

GV 3 -
This point relates to impotence, sciatica, tingling of the hand, muscle degeneration, motor defects, prostatitis, infertility, pains in the lumbar and sacral region.

GV 4 -
This point relates to balding, anemia as a result of bleeding, back pains, lumbago, kidney pains, vaginal discharges, impotence, prostatitis, diarrhea, weakness.

GV 5 -
This point does not serve as a primary point.

GV 6 -
This point does not serve as a primary point.

GV 7 -
This point relates to weak muscle tone (an inability to walk).

GV 8 -
This point relates to disease of the breast.

GV 9 -
This point relates to back pains, overexcitedness, coughing, asthma, rigidity of the spine.

GV 10 -

This point relates to heartburn, coughing, asthma, back and neck pains, boils.

GV 11 -

This point relates to pain in the shoulder blades.

GV 12 -

This point relates to overexcitedness, radiating pain.

GV 13 -

This point relates to loss of balance, tingling of the hand, rigid back, diseases with fever, headaches.

GV 14 -

This point relates to an inability to write (stemming from the brain), skin allergies, balding, aphasia, hypertension, diseases with fever, colds, afternoon fever, asthma, coughing, epilepsy.

GV 15 -

This point relates to weak muscle tone (an inability to walk), a lack of self-control, distorted speech, disease of the breast, sudden loss of voice, epilepsy.

GV 16 -

This point relates to brittleness of the bones, disease of the breast, tingling of the hand.

GV 17 -

This point relates to migraine.

GV 18 -

This point does not serve as a primary point.

GV 19 -

This point does not serve as a primary point.

GV 20 –

This point relates to loss of balance, aphasia, prolapsed rectum, heatstroke, acute heart attack, loss of consciousness, lack of self-control, mental problems, migraine, general itching, prolapsed stomach, prolapsed uterus, blurred vision, tinnitis, headaches, vertigo.

GV 21 –

This point relates to weakness, a drop in energy.

GV 22 –

This point does not serve as a primary point.

GV 23 –

This point relates to weakness, a drop in energy.

GV 24 –

This point relates to pains in the sebaceous glands.

GV 25 –

This point relates to acne vulgaris, weakness, nasal congestion, nosebleeds, loss of consciousness.

GV 26 –

This point relates to acne vulgaris, pain in the tooth socket, loss of consciousness, mental problems, epilepsy, infant convulsions, rigid back, coma.

GV 27 –

This point relates to acne vulgaris.

GV 28 –

This point relates to loss of balance.

The conception/central meridian

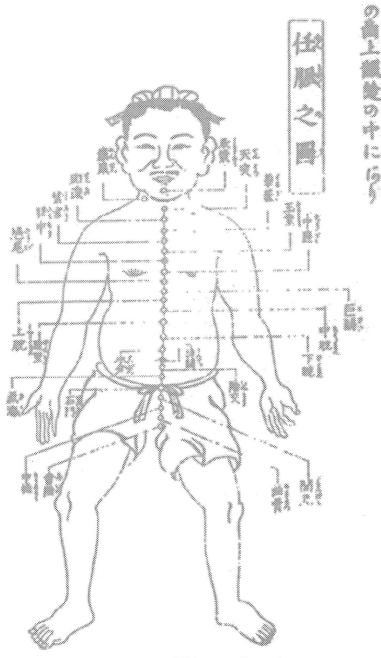

An original Chinese drawing

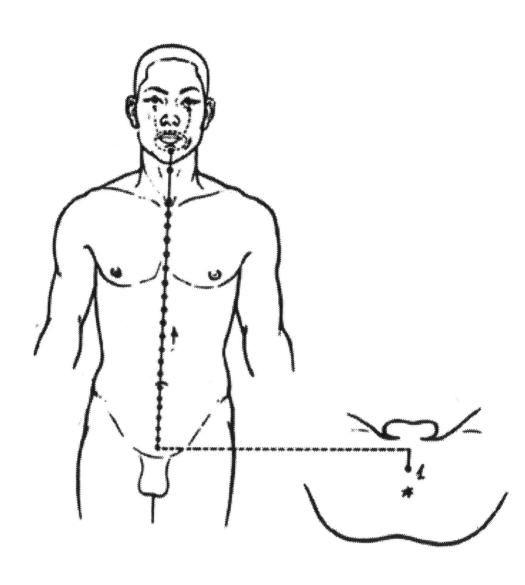

The location of the meridian

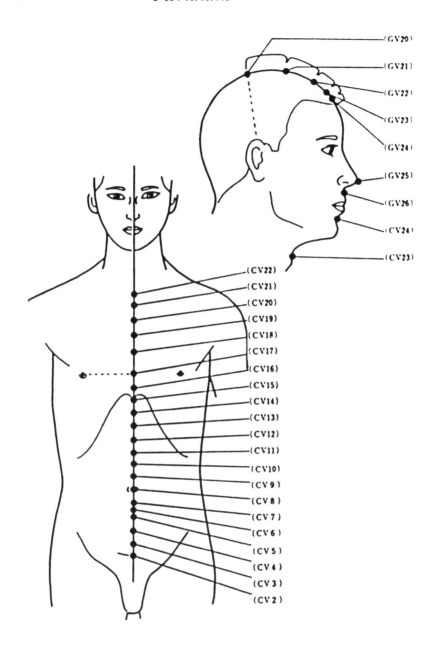

(GV20)
(GV21)
(GV22)
(GV23)
(GV24)
(GV25)
(GV26)
(CV24)
(CV23)

(CV22)
(CV21)
(CV20)
(CV19)
(CV18)
(CV17)
(CV16)
(CV15)
(CV14)
(CV13)
(CV12)
(CV11)
(CV10)
(CV 9)
(CV 8)
(CV 7)
(CV 6)
(CV 5)
(CV 4)
(CV 3)
(CV 2)

The meridian and the points on it

The conception/central meridian
REN-CV (VC)

CV 1 -

This point relates to loss of balance, weakness, after-effects of head injuries, stoppage of urine, low sperm (quantity or quality), drop in energy, inflammation of the uterus lining, anal itching.

CV 2 -

This point relates to pains that stem from a neurological source, prolapsed rectum, hemorrhoids, inflammation of the ovary.

CV 3 -

This point relates to loss of balance, menstrual pains, lack of menstruation, bedwetting, lower abdominal pains, urine incontinence, hot flashes, hypertension, irregular menses, uterine bleeding, vaginal discharges, prolapsed uterus, impotence, defective fertility.

CV 4 -

This point relates to bedwetting, frequent urination, overexcitedness, inflammation of the gallbladder, menstrual pains, irregular menstrual cycle, delay of menses, vaginal discharges, prolapsed uterus, post-natal hemorrhoids, fertility problems.

CV 5 -

This point relates to inflammation of the abdominal muscles, hernia in the groin, uterine bleeding, delay of menses, vaginal discharges, post-natal hemorrhoids, diarrhea, bedwetting, edemas, post-natal bleeding.

CV 6 -

This point relates to stomachaches, lack of menstruation, severe vomiting, weakness, fatigue, diarrhea, constipation, uterine bleeding, vaginal discharges, irregular menstrual cycle, post-natal hemorrhoids, hernia in the groin, abdominal pains.

CV 7 –
This point relates to stomachaches, weakness, drop in energy, hernia in the groin, irregular menstrual cycle, uterine bleeding, vaginal discharges, post-natal hemorrhoids, pains in the navel region.

CV 8 –
This point relates to acute heart attack, hypertension.

CV 9 –
This point relates to hiccups/belching, abdominal pains, edema.

CV 10 –
This point does not serve as a primary point.

CV 11 –
This point relates to yellowness of the skin.

CV 12 –
This point relates to cramping, diarrhea, colitis, vomiting, constipation, diabetes mellitus, heartburn.

CV 13 –
This point relates to stomachache, slow heartbeat.

CV 14 –
This point relates to an obsession with cleanliness, after-effects of a head injury, asthma, hiccups/belching, chest pains, lack of lactation.

CV 15 –
This point relates to disease of the breast.

CV 16 –
This point relates to non-secretion of saliva.

CV 17 –

This point relates to coughing.

CV 18 –

This point relates to underdevelopment of the heart, breathlessness.

CV 19 –

This point relates to pain in the breast, disease of the breast.

CV 20 –

This point relates to underdevelopment of the heart, coughing, breathlessness, chest pains, asthma.

CV 21 –

This point relates to loss of balance.

CV 22 –

This point relates to coughing, breathlessness, inflammation of the throat, loss of voice, sore throat, hiccups/belching.

CV 23 –

This point relates to disease of the lymph glands, pain in the tooth socket, aphasia, functional problems as a result of a stroke, heatstroke, distorted speech, sudden hoarseness, difficulty in swallowing.

CV 24 –

This point relates to the after-effects of a head injury, nausea.

Index of disorders and diseases

Abdominal pain
CV-13, CV-4, CV-7, CV-9, CV-6, CV-12, SP-13, SP-3, SP-4, SP-6, SP-8, ST-25,
ST-34, ST-36, ST-37, ST-44, LI-4, LI-7, LI-11, UB-20, UB-22, UB-25, PC-3,
GB-25, GB-28, GB-39, LIV-13, SI-6

Abnormally low temperature in the limbs
TH-1, TH-3, TH-9, ST-36

Acidity in the stomach
ST-19

Acne vulgaris
GV-25, GV-26, GV-27, TH-22, TH-23, LI-18, LI-20, SI-18, ST-4, ST-11

Acute cystitis
BI-32, BI-33, SP-6, LIV-2, LIV-9, K-5, LIV-8

Acute heart attack
HC-8, GV-20, CV-8

Acute hemorrhoids
ST-3, BI-1, BI-2

After-effects of a head injury
CV-1, CV-14, CV-24

Airsickness
BI-2, ST-36, LI-20, GB-4, GB-16

Alcoholism
ST-13, ST-28, HC-3, GB-20, LIV-10, IG-11, GB-15

Anal itching
CV-1, BI-33, BI-36

Anemia
K-1, K-21, SP-14, SP-19, UB-17, CV-3, CV-4

Aperistalsis (lack of intestinal movement)
ST-36, ST-41, SP-6, LI-11, SI-3, ST-25

Aphasia (inability to speak)
GV-14, GV-20, CV-23, GV-15

Apoplexy (stroke)
BI-28, BI-50, K-17, GV-20, CV-4

Arrhythmia (irregular heartbeat)
LU-5, LU-10, HT-7, K-1, LI-4, ST-36, HC-9

Arthritis of the wrist
LU-6, LU-9, SI-3

Atherosclerosis (hardening of the arteries)
ST-36, ST-45, BI-14

Backache
GV-1, GV-4, GV-9, CV-8, GV-10, UB-10, UB-31-34, UB-28, UB-25, UB-57, UB-58, UB-62, UB-63, PC-5, PC-6

Balding
GV-1, GV-4, GV-14, CV-3

Bedwetting
BI-28, CV-3, CV-4, K-1, SP-6, SP-9, UB-27, UB-28, UB-23

Birth difficulties
UB-67

Blockage of the gall ducts
ST-23, ST-28, SP-6, GB-43, LIV-2, CV-12, CV-14

Blurred vision
K-1, UB-58, UB-60, SI-6, TW-23, GB-14, GB-15, GB-43

Boils
PC-41, GV-10

Breathlessness
CV-18, CV-20, CV-22, LU-1

Brittleness of bone
SP-6, GB-43, GV-16

Bronchial asthma

LU-1, LU-5, LU-6, LU-9, LI-11, ST-11, ST-12, SP-6, SP-21, UB-13, K-3, GV-14,

GV-9, CV-20

Chest pains

CV-7, GV-9, GB-36, GB-39, PC-4, PC-6, PC-7, SI-7, BI-15, HC-6, HT-3

Chest pains while reclining

HT-3, HC-6, HT-7, PC-4, PC-5, PC-7, LIV-14

Colds

UB-12, GV-14

Colitis (inflammation of the large intestine)

CV-12, ST-2, BI-21

Congenital absence of all or part of the brain

BI-2, BI-7, SI-3, SI-19, GB-12

Constipation

CV-12, HT-7, ST-27, SP-4, SP-3, UB-25, UB-28

Cough

CV-17, CV-20, CV-22, BI-16, LU-1, LU-5, LU-6, LU-9, GB-23, TH-15, UB-11, UB-15, K-27, GV-9, GV-10

Cough with blood

UB-13

Cramping
CV-12, SP-4, ST-27

Delay of menses
ST-30, K-12, TH-3, GB-28, SP-6, CV-4

Diabetes mellitus
BI-13, BI-20, ST-36, CV-12, K-1
Diarrhea
ST-25, CV-5, CV-8, CV-12, LI-11, UB-25, UB-22, UB-20, UB-28, GB-25

Difficulties falling asleep
UB-15, UB-62, HT-7, LIV-2, LIV-3, CV-14

Digestive difficulties
LIV-13

Disease of the blood vessels
GV-1, GV-9, TH-8, SI-3

Disease of the breast
CV-15, CV-19, GV-8, GV-15, GV-16

Disease of the lymph glands
CV-23, BI-21, K-1, K-15, LU-9, TH-5

Diseases with fever
ST-44, SI-4, SI-3, UB-12, GB-40, GB-43, GV-13, PC-5, TW-5, TW-3

Dislocation of the shoulder
HC-1, ST-12, ST-14, LI-15, GB-22

Distorted speech
CV-23, CV-24, GV-15

Drop in energy level
GV-21, GV-23, CV-1, CV-7, LU-11, TH-10, TH-14, ST-36

Earache
SI-19

Edema (swelling)
K-7, UB-22, SP-39

Epilepsy
SI-8, K-6, HC-5, HC-6, TW-10, LIV-2, LIV-3, GV-14, GV-15, GV-26

Excessive sweating
K-7, K-11, BI-41, BI-67, LU-1

Exhaustion from illness
GV-21, GV-23, CV-1, CV-6, CV-7, LU-11, TH-10

Eye pains
GB-1, GB-27

Flatulence in the intestines
ST-26, ST-30, GB-25, LIV-12, K-13, SP-6

Fluids in the abdomen following a liver disease
ST-26, ST-30, LIV-12

Fracture of the coccyx
GV-1, BI-31, BI-34

Fracture of the forearm
LU-9, LI-4, LI-11, HT-7, HC-8

Fracture of the lower leg
K-5, LIV-7, ST-36

Frigidity
ST-26, K-7, HC-8

Functional apoplexy
CV-23, BI-2

Gallstones
LIV-14, GB-38, ST-26

Gastritis (inflammation of the stomach)
SI-5, ST-21, ST-41, SP-3

Generalized itching
CV-20, GV-20, SP-21, K-17

Hand tremor
TW-5

Headaches
GB-8, GB-14, GB-15, ST-3, GB-20, UB-7, UB-10, UB-11, SI-3, SI-4, UB-23, UB-64, UB-67, UB-62, TW-3, TW-5, TW-10, GB-1

Hearing difficulties
LI-4, GB-2, SI-19, SI-3, LI-6, ST-7, GB-2

Heartburn
HC-6, BI-14, BI-15, HT-3, GV-10, SP-18, GB-24

Heatstroke
GV-20, CV-23

Hemorrhoids
SP-12, CV-2, GV-1, BI-24, UB-57

Hernia in the groin
LIV-10, GB-28, GV-1, CV-4, CV-5, CV-6, CV-7, ST-30, SP-6, K-6, GB-28

Hiccups/belching
ST-24, ST-29, CV-9, GB-24, LIV-14, CV-17, CV-22

Hoarseness and sudden loss of voice
GV-15, K-1, K-6, HT-4, CV-22, CV-23

Hypertension (high blood pressure)
CV-3, CV-8, GV-14

Impotence
BI-23, BI-32, GV-3, K-3, CV-3, CV-4, SP-6

Inability to produce red blood cells
ST-19, SP-5, SP-9, BI-9

Inability to sleep
LI-2, LI-4, HT-9, SI-3, SI-10, HT-7

Inability to write (stemming from the brain)
GV-14, TH-1, TH-4, SI-9

Infant convulsions
GV-26, UB-63, K-1

Infertility
LIV-3, LIV-8, SP-6, K-13, CV-3, CV-4, GV-3

Inflammation of the abdominal muscles
CV-5, ST-26, GB-26

Inflammation of the eyelid
HT-6, GB-1, TH-23, BI-1

Inflammation of the fallopian tubes
BI-31, GB-26, GB-34, LIV-3, BI-18

Inflammation of the foot joint
BI-60, BI-64, GB-43, LIV-1, ST-44

Inflammation of the gall ducts
ST-36, K-14, K-16, LIV-2

Inflammation of the gallbladder
CV-4, LIV-3, LIV-8, GB-27

Inflammation of the lymph glands
LI-4, ST-36, ST-44

Inflammation of the ovary
SP-12, CV-2, ST-29
Inflammation of the shoulder
HC-1, SI-12, SI-14, SI-15, TH-14, GB-22

Inflammation of the throat
TH-15, CV-22, SP-19

Inflammation of the uterus lining
CV-1, GV-1, GV-2, BI-28

Influenza
UB-12

Irregular menstruation
ST-25, ST-30, SP-6, UB-20, UB-31-34, K-2, K-3, K-5, K-6, LIV-5, GV-3, CV-3, CV-4, CV-6, CV-7

Irritation
LI-4, LU-9, K-1, SP-6, HC-8

Jaw pains
GB-43

Kidney pains
K-17, BI-52, GV-4

Knee joint bursitis
ST-33, ST-36, SP-10, BI-38, BI-40, BI-65, GB-34, GB-39, ST-44

Knock-knee
LIV-9, GB-32, GB-33, ST-36

Lack of lactation
SI-1, SI-2, HT-1, HT-4, LIV-14, CV-17, CV-20, CV-7

Lack of menstruation
SP-6, LIV-3, ST-30, CV-3, CV-6, LI-4, UB-20

Lack of self-control
GV-15, GV-20, BI-9, HT-7
Laryngitis
TH-16, LI-17, SI-15

Leg cramps
LIV-8, ST-36, SP-5

Loss of balance
CV-1, CV-3, CV-21, GV-13, GV-20, GV-28

Loss of consciousness
GV-26, ST-36, GV-20, GV-25, K-1

Low sperm (quantity or quality)
CV-1, GV-2, BI-30, GB-27, SP-12, SP-13, SP-6

Lower back and pelvis pain (pains in the lower back and pelvis)
GV-2, BI-32, BI-35, ST-39, K-3, GB-30, GB-28, GB-27, GB-25

Lumbago (pain in the lower back, hips)
GV-1, GV-2, GV-4, UB-40, GV-26, GB-30, GB-28, GB-27, GB-25, LIV-13

Menstrual pains
SP-6, CV-3, BI-27, BI-32, K-5, SP-10, LIV-8

Mental disturbances
GV-20, GV-26, PC-7

Migraine
GV-17, GV-20, LI-4, HC-4, SI-13, LI-7

Miscarriage
LI-4, SP-6, GV-1

Mood swings
LU-9, LU-5, ST-36, HT-7, UB-15, PC-7

Muscle degeneration
GV-3

Muscle weakness
LU-5, LU-11, LI-4, LI-11, ST-36, SP-3, HT-2, ST-39, ST-40, GB-30, GB-34, GB-37

Nasal congestion
GB-15, UB-7, UB-10, UB-67, GB-20, GV-25, GV-20

Nasal dryness
GV-25, LI-19, GB-1, LI-20, LI-6

Nausea
LI-4, CV-24, GB-5, PC-6, PC-5

Neck pains
TW-10, UB-11, SI-4, SI-3, GV-10, GB-40, GB-36

Neurological syndrome following a stroke
BI-2, SI-7, SI-15

Night sweats
K-7, K-23, UB-13, HT-6, BI-15, GB-17, SI-3, TW-11, TW-14, TW-15

Non-secretion of saliva (non-secretion of saliva)
GV-4, GV-5, CV-16, LI-4, ST-20, ST-24, ST-36, SP-6, SP-15, GB-24, LIV-11

Nosebleed
LI-4, LI-6, LI-20, ST-44, PC-3, UB-60, GV-25

Obesity
LIV-13, GB-25, ST-25

Obsession with cleanliness
HT-7, HC-6, CV-14, BI-17, ST-36, ST-34

Overexcitedness
GV-9, GV-12, CV-4, HT-7

Pain during urination
LIV-8, LIV-5

Pain in the achilles tendon
BI-58, BI-59, BI-60, BI-61, K-4

Pain in the arms
ST-38, BI-57, LI-15, PC-5, LI-6, SI-8

Pain in the bones
GB-22, ST-14, BI-41, BI-26, UB-11

Pain in the bones of the foot
SP-2, SP-7, K-5, BI-60

Pain in the breast
GB-23, CV-19, ST-17, ST-34

Pain in the foot
LIV-2, ST-4, BI-60, ST-44

Pain in the heel
GB-43, ST-41, K-5

Pain in the nape of the neck
SI-8

Pain in the ovaries
ST-36, K-5, SP-8, SP-10, GB-33, BI-39

Pain in the sebaceous (skin) glands
ST-44, GV-14, GV-24

Pain in the shoulder blades
LI-15, TH-14, GV-11

Pain in the thigh
BI-36, BI-56, ST-31, ST-37, GB-32, GB-33, GB-39, LIV-8

Pain in the tooth socket
GV-26, CV-23, ST-2, BI-1, LI-4
Painful menstruation
SP-6, CV-3, BI-27, CV-4, ST-37

Paralysis of the solar plexus
HT-5, HC-6, ST-36, SP-6, LIV-3

Poisoning from eating meat
ST-21, ST-25, SP-15, SI-3, SI-4

Post-natal bleeding
CV-5, CV-6, CV-7
Post-natal hemorrhoids
CV-4, CV-7, CV-6

Premature balding
K-11, K-20, K-27, LU-1, LU-5

Prolapsed rectum
GV-20, LI-20, CV-2

Prolapsed uterus
K-2, K-5, K-6, SP-6, GB-28, LIV-8, GV-20, CV-3, CV-4

Prominent heel
BI-61, BI-63, K-5

Prostatitis (inflammation of the prostate)
GV-3

Quitting smoking
GB-8
Radiating pain
GV-12, ST-36, BI-63

Rigid back
GV-26, GV-13

Sciatica
GV-1, GV-2, GV-3, BI-29, BI-37

Severe vomiting
CV-6, HC-6, ST-36, SP-6, LI-11, SP-4, SP-3, UB-22, UB-21, PC-7, PC-5, PC-6,
GB-24, LIV-13, LIV-14
Skin allergies
LI-11, SP-10, GV-14

Slow heartbeat
HT-9, TH-10, HC-3, CV-13, LI-4, ST-18

Sore throat
LI-4, LI-7, LI-11

Stiff neck
TW-10, UB-11, SI-3, SI-4, LU-7

Stoppage of urine
BI-23, BI-28, BI-32, CV-1

Swelling in the lips and cheeks
LI-4, LI-7, LI-20, ST-3, SI-1, TW-12, GV-26

Tennis elbow
LI-10, LI-11, TH-10, HT-2, HT-3

Tingling of the foot
GV-3, BI-28, BI-36, SP-6

Tingling of the hand
GV-13, GV-16, BI-12, GB-20, TH-2, HT-3

Tonal loss in the blood vessels
LU-9, LIV-2, K-10

Toothache
ST-3, ST-44, ST-7, TW-21, GB-2, GB-37

Underdevelopment of the heart
CV-18, CV-20, K-10, SP-20, HT-2

Urine incontinence
BI-28, CV-3, K-1, UB-27, UB-23, UB-28, SP-9, SP-6, K-6, K-3, LIV-2, LIV-3, CV-3, CV-4, CV-6

Uterine bleeding
LIV-6, LIV-3, CV-3, CV-5, CV-6, CV-7

Vaginal discharges
GB-27, GB-28, UB-23, GV-4, CV-3, CV-4, CV-5, CV-6, CV-7

Vertigo
K-1, UB-7, UB-62, SI-19, GB-20, GV-20

Weak muscle tone (an inability to walk)
GB-34, GB-41, ST-36, ST-42, GV-7, GV-15, ST-36, ST-39, ST-40, SP-6

Weakness
GV-4, GV-21, CV-1, LU-11

Weakness in the heart muscle
LU-1, LU-10, HT-6, HT-9, HC-3

Weakness of the eyes
GB-1, HT-8, ST-2, HT-5, K-5

Yellowness of the skin
LIV-2, LIV-3, CV-11, BG-26